THE CATECHETICAL ORATION
OF ST. GREGORY OF NYSSA

Early Church Classics.

THE CATECHETICAL ORATION OF ST. GREGORY OF NYSSA

BY THE

VEN. J. H. SRAWLEY, D.D.

ARCHDEACON OF WISBECH
RECTOR OF WEETING, NORFOLK

WIPF & STOCK · Eugene, Oregon

Wipf and Stock Publishers
199 W 8th Ave, Suite 3
Eugene, OR 97401

The Catechetical Oration of St. Gregory of Nyssa
By Srawley, J. H.
Softcover ISBN-13: 979-8-3852-0929-3
Hardcover ISBN-13: 979-8-3852-0930-9
eBook ISBN-13: 979-8-3852-0931-6
Publication date 12/6/2023
Previously published by SPCK, 1917

This edition is a scanned facsimile of the original edition published in 1917.

CONTENTS

THE CATECHETICAL ORATION
OF ST. GREGORY OF NYSSA

INTRODUCTION

I. Occasion and Date of the *Catechetical Oration*

THE author of the present treatise, Gregory of Nyssa, was the younger brother of Basil, Bishop of Cæsarea in Cappadocia. The main facts about Gregory's family are stated by himself in his life of his sister Macrina, and the chief incidents in his career are indicated in the introduction to the translation of that book, which is included in the present series of *Early Church Classics*.[1] Gregory was made Bishop of Nyssa in 372 A.D., but he came into prominence as a writer and a theologian on the death of Basil in 379 A.D., and most of his more important works were written subsequent to that date. He played a prominent part in the final events which led to the victory of the Nicene cause at Constantinople in 381 A.D., and was regarded as one of the champions of orthodoxy in the East.[2]

The three Cappadocian Fathers, Basil, Gregory of Nazianzus, and Gregory of Nyssa, were linked together not only by personal ties, but also by common interests.

[1] Gregory of Nyssa, *Life of Macrina*, by the Rev. W. K. Lowther Clarke.

[2] His name was included among the bishops with whom communion was accepted as a test of orthodoxy in the edict of Theodosius.

7

They approached the controversies of the time on the Person of Christ and the doctrine of the Trinity with similar aims, and sought to deal with them on similar lines. Basil was the pioneer, and the two Gregories built upon the foundation which he had laid. To their labours we owe the terminology in which the doctrine of the Trinity came to be finally formulated in Eastern theology.[1]

Another link between the three Cappadocian Fathers is found in their enthusiasm for Origen's writings. Origen was the first philosophical theologian of the Church, and it was to Origen's writings that the three Fathers turned for inspiration and guidance in seeking to commend the Christian faith to the best culture of their time. Lastly, the interest of Basil in the ascetic and monastic movement was shared by the two Gregorys, and this interest finds expression in the early work of Gregory of Nyssa, *On Virginity*, and in his *Life of Macrina*.[2]

The *Catechetical Oration* is one of the later works of Gregory of Nyssa. At the beginning of Chap. XXXVIII the author refers his readers for a further exposition of his teaching on faith to other treatises, in which, he says, "we have not only engaged in controversy with our opponents, but we have also independently considered the questions proposed to us." This passage seems to contain an allusion to his great work *Against Eunomius*, the leader of the Anomœan (or extreme Arian) party, and possibly also to his discourse *On the Deity of the Son and of the Holy Spirit*. The former of these Jerome heard read by Gregory of Nyssa, in the presence of Gregory of Nazianzus, at Constantinople in 381 A.D.[3] Possibly it

---

[1] See article "Cappadocian Theology" in Hastings' *Encyclopædia of Religion and Ethics*.

[2] On the monasteries of Pontus see W. K. Lowther Clarke's edition of Gregory of Nyssa, *Life of Macrina*, in the present series.

[3] Jerome, *de Vir. Ill.* c. 128.

was only a portion of the work (which is the longest of all Gregory's treatises and is in twelve books) that Jerome heard read, in which case the completed work may be dated a year or two later. The discourse *On the Deity of the Son and the Holy Spirit* was delivered at Constantinople in 383 A.D. The *Catechetical Oration* may have been written a few years later, but probably not much later, as the danger from Anomœan teaching is still present to his mind.

The *Catechetical Oration* is designed as a manual for the use of catechists, in order to assist them in their task of instructing educated converts during their preparation for baptism. It deals with current objections to the Christian faith, and its aim throughout is practical. But in dealing with these objections Gregory touches on the leading doctrines of the faith and unfolds in its broad outlines the theological system to which he himself had been led. The details of this system may be filled in by reference to his other theological works which throw light upon, and complete, the outline given in the present treatise. The more important of these works are as follows—

1. *Against Eunomius.* This deals with the whole Arian position.

2. *On " Not Three Gods,"* and *To the Greeks, Of Universal Ideas.* These expound the doctrine of the Trinity and refute the charge of tritheism brought against it.

3. *Antirrhetic against Apollinaris.* In this work Gregory expounds against Apollinaris the doctrine of the Incarnation, and deals with the reality of the two natures in Christ, and the manner of their union.

4. *On the Making of Man,* and *On the Soul and the Resurrection.* These works are of a more distinctly philosophical character and exhibit Gregory's views on the constitution of human nature, the Fall, and the ultimate destiny of man.

The *Catechetical Oration* contains four distinct sections. In the first (Prologue, Chaps. I–IV) Gregory deals with

the doctrine of the Trinity. In the second section (Chaps.
V–VIII) he expounds the creation of man, the origin of
evil, and the Fall. The third section (Chaps. IX–XXXII)
contains Gregory's treatment of the doctrines of the
Incarnation and Redemption, and deals with current
objections. The final section of the book is devoted to
the Sacraments of Baptism and the Eucharist, and the
indispensable conditions (faith and moral amendment)
which are associated with them.[1]

The period to which the *Catechetical Oration* belongs
was well suited for such an exposition of the Christian
faith as that which it presents. The victory over Arian-
ism which followed on the accession of Theodosius prepared the way for a constructive presentation of the faith
and a review of the whole series of questions which
divided the allegiance of Christians or deterred out-
siders from accepting Christianity. The opponents to
whom Gregory refers are of various kinds, Jews and
Pagans, Arians and Manichæans. In treating of the
doctrine of the Trinity, Gregory has in view Jewish mono-
theism and Greek polytheism. Both here and in the
later chapters on Baptism and Faith he also shows the in-
adequacy of the Arian teaching, represented by Eunomius.
In his exposition of creation, the Fall, and the origin of
evil, he combats the theories of the Manichæans, whose
dualistic teaching rendered necessary the vindication of
the providence of GOD and the free-will of man.

In dealing with these various problems Gregory shows
great versatility of mind and considerable acumen. His
style is often obscure and difficult to render in English.
In the present edition the translator has received valuable

---

[1] In the Paris editions of Gregory and in some late MSS.
there is added to the concluding words of the treatise some
lines which are undoubtedly spurious and form no part of
the true text. They are an extract from a work on the
Incarnation by Theodore of Rhaithu, a writer of the seventh
century.

help from Mr. F. H. Colson, late Fellow of St. John's College, Cambridge, who has kindly read through the translation and offered useful suggestions. He is also indebted to the Syndics of the Cambridge University Press for permission to make occasional use of material contained in the Introduction and Notes to the edition of the *Catechetical Oration* which he prepared for the series of *Cambridge Patristic Texts* in 1903.

The *Catechetical Oration* was a favourite work with later theologians of the Greek Church. It is quoted by Theodoret in his Dialogues (cent. v), and by Leontius of Byzantium (cent. vi) in his treatise against Nestorius and Eutyches. John of Damascus (cent. viii) in his great work *On the Orthodox Faith* borrows largely from the chapters on the Trinity and on the Eucharist, as also does a later Byzantine theologian, Euthymius Zigabenus (cent. xii). Gregory's chapter on the Eucharist is also quoted in the same century in the account of the discussion which took place between Nerses, the Catholicos of Armenia, and Theorian, who was sent by the Emperor in 1170 to win over the Armenians to the orthodox faith. But a fuller study of Gregory's treatise, and the presence in it of some of the more doubtful speculations of Origen (*e. g.* his teaching on the final restoration of all souls), awakened suspicions in orthodox circles. Germanus, Patriarch of Constantinople in the seventh century, in a work which Photius had seen, refers to these suspicions and suggests that the works of Gregory had been interpolated by the Origenists, a suggestion for which there is no adequate justification.

2. Gregory of Nyssa as a Theologian

Though the aim of the *Catechetical Oration* is to offer practical guidance to Christian catechists in the instruction of converts to the faith, it abounds in philosophic thought, and the author attempts, within the limits

imposed upon him by his task, to establish the truth of
Christianity by rational considerations and with the
help of contemporary thought. To this fact the treatise
owes its main interest. The attempt to present a reasoned
view of GOD and the universe on the basis of the truths
of the Christian religion was a natural outcome of the
contact of the Greek mind with Christianity, and in this
sense it is true that Greek patristic theology was "the
last characteristic creation of the Greek genius." The
Greek apologists of the second century had attempted
within a limited range the task of reconciling Christianity
with Greek philosophy. It was attempted again with
far greater boldness and largeness of design by Clement
of Alexandria and Origen. The latter was the first great
philosopher of the Church, and his speculations covered
the whole field of the religious problems of his time. In
the subsequent period Origen's influence was widespread.
All the great defenders of orthodoxy in the fourth century,
as well as many of the leaders of the various heresies,
were more or less disciples of Origen, whose influence is
shown not so much in the doctrines which they borrow
from him as in the spirit and method of their teaching.
Among the fathers of the fourth century the three Cap-
padocians were conspicuous for their devotion to Origen's
writings, and this devotion is shown in the case of Basil
and Gregory of Nazianzus by their compilation of the
Philocalia, a series of extracts from Origen's writings.
But in speculative interest, in the wide range of problems
discussed by him, and in the extent of his indebtedness
to Origen, Gregory of Nyssa surpasses them both.

The influence of Origen on Gregory of Nyssa is shown
in the *Catechetical Oration* in the very idea of illustrating
the truths of Christianity from contemporary thought,[1]

[1] See, *e. g.*, his reference to "general ideas" at the beginning of Chap. V, and his representation of the doctrine
of the Trinity as the mean between Judaism and Hellenism
(Chap. III).

and in the appeal which he makes to human reason as an authority in support of Christian doctrines.[1] Origen's influence appears again in Gregory's resort in two passages (Chaps. VIII, XXXII) to the allegorical interpretation of Scripture,[2] and is shown in a still more convincing manner in his whole treatment of the Divine providence in relation to the world-process, which culminates in the final absorption of all created things in the unity of GOD. In this connexion, like Origen, Gregory assigns an important place to man's free-will, which renders possible the declension of man from the path of virtue which he was meant to pursue.

According to Gregory (who here follows Origen and is in accord with the teaching of most of the Platonist Fathers of the Church), evil has no substantive existence, but arises from the act of the will in refusing the good and deliberately turning away from light (Chaps. V, VI, p. 37 f.). But the discord arising from evil cannot finally defeat GOD's purpose. GOD must eventually be "all in all." The purpose of the Incarnation is to restore all created beings to a state of final harmony with GOD. Satan himself will one day be redeemed and led to own the saving work of the Creator (Chap. XXVI, p. 81 f.). For those who lack the grace of baptism there is prepared the "refiner's fire" after

[1] In his expository work *On the Life of Moses*, written in old age, Gregory urges the importance of the help which may be gained in the pursuit of the higher life by an alliance with all that is best in the learning and philosophy of the non-Christian world (*de Vita Moysis*, in Migne, *P. G.*, xliv. 336).

[2] In the time of Gregory allegorism was beginning to fall into disrepute, as the exigencies of controversy had shown the need of a more literal and scientific interpretation. Basil especially shows a reserve in his use of it, but Gregory defends and freely uses allegory in his other works. In Chap. XXXII. of the present treatise he expounds its principles and says, "In the Gospel all words and actions have a higher and more divine meaning, and there is nothing . . . which does not reveal itself as a kind of mixture of the divine with the human element."

the resurrection (Chap. XXXV, p. 105 f.), and then there will arise from all creation "a chorus of praise" (Chap. XXVI, p. 82). This following of Origen in some of his most daring speculations imperilled Gregory's reputation for orthodoxy in later days and led to the suggestion that his works had been interpolated by the Origenists.

But Gregory is no slavish follower of Origen. At times he modifies Origen's views, and in the light of fuller experience corrects his conclusions. He rejects Origen's theory of the pre-temporal creation of all souls, and also his view that the body was only assigned to man after the Fall and as a punishment of sin. According to Gregory the creation of man was designed from the first by GOD as a means of realizing the union of the worlds of intelligence and sense, which for him, as for Origen, constituted the two factors in the existing order of things (Chap. VI, p. 38 f.). The "coats of skin" in Genesis iii, which Origen had interpreted to mean the body, are explained by Gregory as the condition of mortality which was appointed by GOD as a merciful provision for undoing the effects of the Fall, by resolving man into his constituent elements, and so refashioning his nature and freeing it from the evil in which it had been involved (Chap. VIII, p. 46). This conception shows Gregory's indebtedness to Methodius, a writer of the third century, who in his day had figured as an opponent of Origen. Gregory's acquaintance with the writings of this author are shown further in his realistic conception of the effects of the Incarnation, which resulted, according to him, in the assumption of humanity as a whole by the Word. As the principle of death spread from Adam to the whole of humanity, so the resurrection of Christ became for humanity a principle of life (Chaps. XVI, XXXV, pp. 64, 103). The starting-point of this conception is, of course, the language of Rom. v. 15 f., but the realistic manner in which it is conceived, and the particular conception of humanity as a unity, are characteristic of Methodius.

In his treatment of the Incarnation and the objections raised against it Gregory shows himself indebted to Athanasius, and like that Father, he attempts to answer the question " Why did GOD become man? " He adopts many of the arguments of Athanasius, and appeals to the facts of the Gospel history and the progress of the Church as a proof of the Divine origin of the Christian religion (Chaps. XII, XIII, XVIII). Like Athanasius he justifies the Incarnation by an appeal to the immanence of GOD in Creation, and deals with the necessity of the death of Christ, and its manner, the crucifixion (Chaps. XXV, XXXII). But here, again, Gregory shows at times his independence of thought. Thus in treating of the death of Christ he argues that death was necessary in order that Christ might share in all the experiences of humanity (Chap. XXXII, p. 92), and in answering the difficulty that GOD might have redeemed man by assuming a body more worthy of the Divine indwelling than that taken from human nature, he urges the transcendence of GOD, which exalts Him above all created things alike, so that there is no more dishonour in His association with one form of created existence than another (Chap. XXVII, p. 85). In its general treatment of the Incarnation, however, Gregory's treatise compares unfavourably with that of Athanasius *On the Incarnation*. According to Athanasius the purpose of the Incarnation was twofold, to restore man to union with GOD by delivering him from sin and corruption, and to revive in him the knowledge of GOD. The former of these conceptions, with its emphasis on "life" and "immortality," its insistence on the "deification" of man, and its realistic conception of the unity of humanity in Christ, is characteristic of Greek theology, and shows the Platonist and somewhat pantheistic colouring of the Christian thought of the period. In Gregory of Nyssa it receives additional emphasis from his almost complete neglect of the second aspect of the Incarnation on which Athanasius insists,

the recovery of the knowledge of GOD by man. From
it proceeds Gregory's teaching on the Sacraments which
are the " extension " in the life of the individual of that
process of " deification," or the raising of man to union
with the Divine life, which it was the purpose of the Incarnation to effect (Chaps. XXXV, XXXVII, pp. 101, 108).

In another respect Gregory compares unfavourably with
Athanasius. His treatment of the Atonement of Christ
(Chaps. XX–XXIV), which is one of the most original
features of the treatise, is for the modern reader one of
the most repellent, and is in striking contrast with the
more profound and reverent treatment of the question
by Athanasius. Gregory finds in the work of redemption an exhibition of the attributes of GOD, power, wisdom,
goodness, and justice. Goodness inspired GOD with the
desire to rescue man; wisdom suggested the means;
the Divine power was shown in the greatness of the condescension which enabled GOD to assume human nature;
the method of redemption was an exhibition of the Divine
justice. As man had freely surrendered himself to Satan,
it was impossible, without injustice, to rescue him by force.
Hence a ransom was necessary, and a ransom which the
master of him who had been enslaved was willing to
accept. Attracted by the miracles of Christ, Satan was
led to accept Him as the ransom. But the veil of the
humanity hid from the adversary the Deity of Christ,
and thus he who had originally deceived mankind was
himself in turn deceived—an act of retribution and strict
justice, so Gregory maintains, the justification of which
he finds in its beneficent purpose. For Satan himself
will finally benefit by it and be brought within reach
of the redemptive work of God. This conception of a
ransom paid to Satan Gregory derived from Origen.[1]

[1] The Gnostic, Marcion, still earlier, appears to have
regarded the death of Christ as a ransom, by which the good
God purchased mankind from the creator of the world (the
Demiurge). See Harnack, *Hist. of Dogma* (Eng. tr.), I. 273.

The idea of an act of deception practised on Satan through the veiling of the Deity by the humanity of Christ is found in Gregory of Nazianzus,[1] who, however, repudiates with scorn the notion of a ransom paid to Satan. Gregory's whole conception appears in a still more crude and repellent form in his contemporary, Amphilochius of Iconium.[2] It is repeated by later writers in both East and West, and lingered on until the time of Anselm, who in his *Cur deus homo* finally gave it its *coup de grâce*. It is startling to find this strange piece of mythology, which sounds like an echo of crude popular theology, in the treatise of a cultured and thoughtful writer like Gregory. But a fuller study of his writings suggests that it is not a central or leading part of his teaching on redemption. He nowhere dwells on the thought of Christ's death as a sacrifice to God or as an act of propitiation. His central thought is that redemption is found in the restoration of man to the Divine life through the union of the two natures in Christ, and in that respect Gregory is a typical representative of the general trend of Greek theology.

The *Catechetical Oration* contains few echoes of the larger controversies which filled so large a place in the history of Gregory's time. His treatment of the doctrine of the Trinity in the opening chapters summarises the doctrine of Athanasius as formulated by the Cappadocian Fathers. But he had already dealt in detail with the Arian position in earlier works.[3] In the later chapters (XXXVIII, XXXIX) of the *Catechetical Oration* he shows the importance of a right faith in order to ensure the efficacy of baptism, and, like Athanasius before him,[4] he insists that the belief in a created Son and Spirit can only impair the character of the new life in baptism, because it brings the convert into union with the creature instead of the Creator.

[1] *Or.*, xxxix. 13.
[2] See Holl, *Amphilochius v. Ikonium*, pp. 98 f.
[3] See p. 8.　　　　[4] *Or.*, ii. *c. Ar.* 42.

B

Reference has already been made to the influence of Platonism upon Gregory's thought. Much of this influence is undoubtedly indirect, and is part of the debt which Gregory owes to Origen and the current philosophy of the time; but in many places Gregory seems to show direct acquaintance with the *Timaeus* and other treatises of Plato. Like the Neoplatonists, Gregory affirms the mystery of the Divine Being. We can attain only "a moderate degree of apprehension of the knowledge of GOD" (Chap. III). But GOD may be known mediately through His energies and operations (*Prol.*). It is above all in the human soul that we may find the mirror of GOD. Hence Gregory illustrates the doctrine of the Trinity from the psychology of human nature (Chap. III). Elsewhere he illustrates the affinity of human nature with the Divine by Plato's illustration of the eye, which he represents as attracting the light by virtue of the elements of light contained in it (Chap. V, p. 35). Other Platonist features in the *Catechetical Oration* are the conception of the negative character of evil, the purification of souls, the treatment of the immanence of GOD in the universe; the realism of Gregory's conception of the unity of humanity, a feature which appears in a more pronounced form in his treatise in defence of the doctrine of the Trinity, *On " Not Three Gods " ;* lastly, his whole conception of the Incarnation as a cosmical act, the end of which is to restore all spiritual beings to union with GOD.

Gregory's chapter on the Eucharist, on the other hand, shows his acquaintance with the terminology and ideas of Aristotle. On the latter's theory of nutrition and his distinction of "form" and "matter" he builds an ingenious theory to explain the transformation of the elements of bread and wine in the Eucharist into the Body and Blood of Christ (Chap. XXXVII). As food and drink are changed into the human body by digestion, and were so changed in the human body assumed by the Word, so now, no longer through eating, but immediately, by the power of the Word, the bread and wine are changed into His Body and His Blood, the constituent elements ($\sigma\tau o\iota\chi\epsilon\hat{\iota}a$) of the bread and wine being arranged under a new " form " ($\epsilon\hat{\iota}\delta o\varsigma$), the Body and Blood of Christ. This theory is of the nature of an illustration only, and moves in a different circle of ideas from the later Western doctrine of Transubstantiation. Gregory teaches a " qualitative unity " between the elements and the sacred realities with which they are associated, not an actual identity or change of " substance." The later teaching of the Greek Church advanced upon Gregory's teaching by maintaining, as does John of Damascus, the complete identity of the consecrated elements with the Body and the Blood of Christ, and affirming that the Eucharistic body is identical with the historical body of Christ.

In the *Catechetical Oration* the apologetic and speculative interest tends to predominate over the ethical interest. But Gregory has a profound sense of the moral glory of the Incarnation, as an exhibition of the love of GOD and consistent with, and worthy of, His moral nature. To him it is a sufficient answer to all objections to say that it was a task worthy of GOD to succour the needy. That His power could stoop so low was a greater miracle than any of the wonders of Creation. Nor is Gregory unmindful of the moral demands of the Christian life. In his realistic conception of the Eucharist he still insists on faith, and in his concluding chapter he sets forth the need of moral effort and amendment of life in order to make effective the new birth of baptism. Where these are lacking, " though it be a bold thing to say, yet I will say it and not draw back; in such cases the water is water, and the gift of the Holy Spirit nowhere appears in what takes place."

The review which has been given above shows the many various elements which Gregory has assimilated from earlier and contemporary thought, both Christian and non-Christian, as well as his own originality and speculative bent of mind. A keen interest in metaphysical problems, an endeavour to understand and come to terms with the best non-Christian thought of the age, lastly a profound conviction of the power of the Christian religion to satisfy the intellectual and moral needs of man, these are the features which give a living interest to the *Catechetical Oration* and make it instructive reading to-day.

3. EDITIONS AND TEXT

The earliest edition of the Greek text of the works of Gregory of Nyssa was published at Paris in 1615 in two volumes, the editor being the Jesuit, Fronto Ducæus. A second edition in three volumes was published by Morel at Paris in 1638. It was a reprint of the earlier edition, but included the Appendix of Gretser (containing some additional treatises), which had been published in 1618. The work appears to have been carelessly done, and the text is very corrupt and contains many lacunae. Between the end of the seventeenth century and the middle of the nineteenth century various unedited works of Gregory were printed in the patristic collections of Zacagni,[1] Gallandi,[2] and Cardinal Mai,[3] and the greater part of this material was reprinted in the three volumes of Gregory's works which find a place in Migre's *Patrologia graeca* (xliv–xlvi, Paris, 1858).

The first scholar of the nineteenth century who applied himself to a critical study of the text of Gregory was J. G. Krabinger, who, with the help of manuscripts in the Royal Library at Munich, produced amended texts of a few treatises, including the *Catechetical Oration*.[4]

[1] L. A. Zacagni, *Collectanea monumentorum veterum ecclesiae graecae ac latinae* (Rome, 1698).

[2] A. Gallandi, *Bibliotheca veterum patrum* (Venice, 1765–1781).

[3] Cardinal Mai, *Scriptorum veterum nova collectio* (Rome, 1825 onwards); and *Nova patrum bibliotheca* (Rome, 1847).

[4] *De Anima et Resurrectione* (Leipzig, 1837); *Oratio Catechetica* and *Oratio funebris in Meletium* (Munich, 1838); *de Precatione Orationes* v. (Landshut, 1840).

Krabinger was followed by G. H. Forbes [1] and by F. Oehler,[2] both of whom contemplated complete critical editions of the works of Gregory, but in neither case did their labours extend beyond a single volume. The *Catechetical Oration* is included in an earlier edition of some treatises of Gregory published by Oehler, with a German translation, in 1858,[3] but no fresh study of manuscripts appears to have been undertaken for this edition.

Krabinger's text of the *Catechetical Oration* had the merit of restoring the lacunae, and removing many of the corruptions, which were found in the Paris edition. But it was based on a very limited number of MSS., and these mostly of a late date. A more extended collation of the MSS. was undertaken by the present writer in the years 1900–1903, and a revised text was published in an edition of the treatise for the *Cambridge Patristic Texts* in 1903.[4] For this edition eleven new MSS., in addition to the three MSS. used by Krabinger, were collated or examined, as well as several MSS. which contained the extracts from the treatise found in the *Panoplia Dogmatica* of Euthymius Zigabenus.

The MSS. fall into two main groups. The primary authorities in the first group are : (1) a MS. of about the eleventh century in the Library of St. Mark at Venice (cod. lxvii, cited as *p* in the above edition ; (2) a MS. of the eleventh century in the Vatican Library at Rome (Pii. II, cod. gr. 4, cited as *n*). In the second group the primary authority is a MS. in the British Museum of the tenth or eleventh century (Add. 22509, cited as *f*). The

---

[1] *Gregorii Nysseni . . . quae supersunt omnia . . . recensuit . . . G. H. Forbesius,* Fasc. 1–2 (Burntisland, 1855–1861).

[2] *S. Gregorii ep. Nysseni opera, ex recensione Fr. Oehler,* T. 1 (Halle, 1865).

[3] *Bibliothek der Kirchenväter. II. Theil. Gregor v. Nyssa* (Leipzig, 1858).

[4] *The Catechetical Oration of Gregory of Nyssa.* Edited by J. H. Srawley (Cambridge University Press, 1903).

text of two other MSS. in the British Museum (Royal 16 D i, cent. xiii, cited as *l*; and Royal 16 D xi, cent. xiv, cited as *m*) exhibits many of the distinctive readings of the Paris editions, and is a late and corrupt recension of the text which *f* exhibits in an earlier and purer stage of transmission. On the whole, allowing for an occasional tendency to revision and paraphrase, the text supported by *f* or *f l* commends itself generally as superior to that represented by the former of the two groups described above.

A subsidiary source of evidence for the text is supplied by the quotations from the *Catechetical Oration* found in later Greek writers.

*   *   *   *   *   *   *

The following books on Gregory of Nyssa will be found useful to English readers—

Dictionary of Christian Biography, vol. ii, art. " Gregorius Nyssenus."

Harnack, *History of Dogma*, Eng. tr., vols. iii. and iv.

Hastings' *Encyclopædia of Religion and Ethics*, vol. iii, art. " Cappadocian Theology."

Wace and Schaff, *A Select Library of Nicene and Post-Nicene Fathers*. Vol. v. *Gregory of Nyssa*. The Introduction contains a valuable discussion of Gregory's place in the history of theology.

PROLOGUE

[The importance and the methods of catechetical teaching. Arguments for the existence and unity of GOD.]

CATECHETICAL teaching is necessary for the ministers of the "mystery of godliness," [1] that the Church may be increased by the addition of those who are being saved,[2] while the "word of faith in accordance with the teaching" [3] is brought within reach of the hearing of unbelievers. Yet the same method of teaching will not be suitable in the case of all who come to hear the word, but as the forms of religion vary, so also the instruction must be adapted to meet them, the same object in teaching being kept in view, but different arguments being used in each case. For he who follows the Jewish religion starts from one set of preconceptions, and he who is born and bred in Hellenism starts from another; while the Anomœan, the Manichæan, and the followers of Marcion, Valentinus, Basilides, and the rest who are included in the list of those who are astray in heresy, each have their own preconceptions, and make it necessary to combat their opinions; for the character of the malady must determine also the method of treatment to be applied. You will not apply the same remedy to the polytheism of the Greek as you apply to the Jew's disbelief in the Only-begotten GOD,[4] nor will you in the case of those who

---

[1] 1 Tim. iii. 16.   [2] Cp. Acts ii. 47.   [3] Titus i. 9.
[4] μονογενῆ θεόν. This reading is found in place of "Only-begotten Son" in some important MSS. in John i. 18. The reading is common in both orthodox and Arian writers in the fourth century.

23

have gone astray among heresies use the same arguments in each case to overthrow their erroneous fancies concerning the doctrines of religion. For the arguments which might restore to the right path the Sabellian will not help the Anomœan, nor does the controversy with the Manichæan benefit the Jew, but, as we have said, we must look to men's preconceptions, and adapt our discussion to suit the error in which each is involved, propounding in each discussion certain principles and reasonable propositions, in order that by means of what is admitted on both sides the truth may be unfolded in logical sequence.

When then a discussion arises with one who is attached to Greek ways of thinking, it will be well to begin the argument as follows. Does he presuppose the existence of GOD, or does he agree with the doctrine of the atheists? If he denies the existence of GOD, then by the signs of skill and wisdom shown in the ordering of the universe he will be led to acknowledge therein the existence of some power manifest in created things and transcending the universe. But if, while not denying the existence of GOD, he is led astray by his notions to believe in a plurality of gods, let us have recourse, in dealing with him, to some such argument as this. Does he consider the Deity to be perfect or imperfect? If, as he probably will do, he testifies to the perfection of the Divine nature, let us require him to grant that this perfection extends through everything that is observed in the Deity, in order that the Divine being may not be considered to be a mixture of contrary elements, imperfection and perfection. But whether it be in respect of power, or the conception of goodness, or wisdom, incorruption, eternity, and any other thought worthy of GOD that may happen to be connected with the subject of our inquiry, he will agree, as the logical outcome of this course of reasoning, that perfection is in every case the idea contemplated in the Divine nature.

And when this is admitted, it will be no longer difficult

to bring round his thought, which he has dissipated over a plurality of gods, to confess a single Deity. For if he grants that perfection in every respect is admitted in the Being of whom we speak, but maintains that there are many of these perfect entities exhibiting the same characteristics, it is absolutely necessary, in the case of beings who are distinguished by no variation, but possess the same attributes, that he should either show that which is peculiar to each, or, if thought grasps nothing in the way of peculiarity where no distinguishing feature exists, give up the assumption of such distinction. For if a man finds no such difference either in respect of more and less—because the idea of perfection does not admit of diminution—or any difference in respect to inferiority or superiority—for a being with reference to whom the term "inferior" is not excluded, could no longer be supposed to be GOD—or in respect to what is "ancient" and "modern"—for that which does not always exist lies outside the conception of Deity—but the idea of Godhead is one and the same, and reason discovers no particularity in any respect, the mistaken fancy of a plurality of gods must of necessity be compelled to acknowledge the unity of the Godhead. For if goodness and justice, wisdom and power, are ascribed to it in an equal degree, and incorruption, eternity, and every idea consistent with piety are treated in the same way, since all difference in every respect is eliminated, the plurality of gods is of necessity at the same time eliminated from his belief, and the identity observed throughout brings him round to believe in the unity.

CHAPTER I

[The Christian doctrine of God defended against Judaism. The existence of the Logos.]

BUT since the doctrine of our religion is able to recognise a distinction of persons [1] in the unity of nature, in order that, while contending against the Greeks, our argument may not drift into Judaism, it is fitting in turn that we should correct the error in this respect also by making use of a skilful distinction. For even those who are strangers to our doctrine do not conceive of the Deity as without a Word, and this admission of theirs will make our argument sufficiently clear. For he who admits that GOD is not without a Word will certainly agree that a being who is not without a Word possesses a Word. But we use the same term to express the human word. If, then, our opponent says that he forms his idea of the Word of GOD on the analogy of our human words, he will in this way be led on to the higher conception. For we must of necessity believe that the Word corresponds with the nature, as everything else does. For in humanity there is perceived a certain kind of power and life and wisdom;

---

[1] ὑποστάσεων. As a theological term the word ὑπόστασις was originally used as a possible equivalent to οὐσία ("being," or "existence"), as being the *substratum* or underlying existence of things. Cp. Heb. i. 3 ("the express image of His *being*" (ὑποστάσεως)). It was still used in this sense in the earlier years of the fourth century. But later the two terms were distinguished, and currency was given to this distinction by the formula of the Cappadocian Fathers to denote the Trinity "One being" (οὐσία) "in three persons" (ὑποστάσεις). The later Western term "person" has different associations from ὑπόστασις, which denotes "a particular centre of being."

yet this identity of terms would not lead any one to suppose that the life, or power, or wisdom in the case of GOD are of the same character, but the significations of such expressions are lowered to correspond with the measure of our nature. For since our nature is corruptible and weak, therefore its life is fleeting, its power is unsubstantial, its word is unstable. But in the case of the transcendent nature, along with the greatness of the object contemplated, every statement predicated of it receives a higher significance. So then, even if we speak of GOD's Word, it will not be thought to have its subsistence in the impulse of him who speaks, then passing out of existence, like our speech; but just as our nature, being perishable, has a speech which is perishable, so the incorruptible and ever-existent nature has a Word which is eternal and substantial.

If, then, the course of reasoning leads to the admission that the Word of GOD subsists eternally it must necessarily be admitted that the subsistence of the Word is endowed with life. For it is contrary to piety to think that the Word subsists in an inanimate state, like stones. But if it subsists, being a thing capable of thought and immaterial, it certainly has life, whereas if it is deprived of life, it as certainly does not subsist at all. But we have shown that it is irreverent to suppose that the Word of GOD is unsubstantial. It follows, therefore, that it was shown at the same time that this Word possesses life. And since the nature of the Word is with good reason believed to be simple, and shows itself as having neither a double nor composite character, the Word cannot be considered as living by a participation in life; for such a conception, maintaining that the one exists in the other, would not exclude the idea of a composite character. But once we admit its simplicity, we must think of the Word as having life in itself, not as participating in life.

If, then, the Word lives, seeing it is life, it has also beyond doubt the faculty of will, for no living being is without will. Further, that this will possesses power is an inference which accords with piety. For the refusal to admit such power, will certainly establish its want of power. But such want of power is far removed from our conception of the Deity. For nothing incongruous is observed in the Divine nature, and we must admit that the power of the Word is equal to its purpose, in order that no mixture or concurrence of opposites may be contemplated in the Divine nature, seeing that both want of power and power would be found in the same purpose, if it were capable of one thing and incapable of another. And we must further admit that the will of the Word, though capable of everything, has no inclination to anything that is evil (for the impulse to evil is foreign to the Divine nature), but whatever is good, that also it wills, and seeing that it wills it, it is also certainly capable of performing it, and being capable it is not inoperative, but translates into action every purpose of good. Now the universe is good, and all that is in it is seen to bear the marks of wisdom and skill. All things, therefore, are the works of the Word Who lives and subsists, because He is the Word of GOD, and is endowed with will because He lives, and is able to do all that He chooses, and chooses absolutely what is good and wise and everything else that denotes excellence.

The universe, then, is admitted to be something good, and it has been shown by what we have been saying that the universe is the work of the Word, who not only chooses, but is capable of carrying into effect what is good; and this Word is distinct from Him Whose Word He is—for in a way this term also is a relative term, seeing that along with the Word there is certainly implied also the Father of the Word, for there cannot be a word which is not the word of some one. If, then, the mind of our hearers, owing to the relative character of the term, distinguishes between the Word Himself, and Him from Whom He is derived, there will be no longer any danger of our religion, in its controversy with Greek conceptions, agreeing with those who advocate the tenets of Judaism. On the contrary, it will equally escape the absurdity of either, seeing that it acknowledges that the living Word [1] is both active and creative, which the Jew does not admit, and also that there is no difference in nature between the Word Himself and Him from Whom He is derived.

For just as in our own case we say that the word proceeds from the mind, though it is not entirely the same as the mind, nor altogether different—for because it proceeds from the mind it is other than the mind and not identical with it, but because it manifests the mind, it does not follow that it is conceived of as something distinct from it, but though in nature one with the mind, it is distinct as a subject [2]—so also the Word of GOD, because He has an existence of His own, is distinct from Him from Whom He has His existence; and because He manifests in Himself the attributes which are observed in God, He is identical in nature with Him Who is discerned by the same characteristics. For whether it be goodness or power or wisdom or eternal existence, or the fact that He is incapable of evil, death, and corruption, or that He is perfect in every respect, or anything else of the kind that is made an indication of the way of apprehending the Father, by the same indications the Word Who derives His subsistence from Him will be discovered.

[1] Heb. iv. 5, understood by many Fathers to refer to the personal Word.
[2] The idea is that the " word " is one " subject " and the " mind " another.

CHAPTER II

[*The same continued. The existence of the Spirit.*]

JUST as, by a process of ascent [1] from the facts of our
own nature, we arrived at a knowledge of the Word in
the transcendent nature, in the same way we shall be
led to the conception of the Spirit by contemplating
in our own nature certain shadows and resemblances of
the ineffable Power. But in our case the spirit (or
breath) [2] is the drawing in of the air, an element foreign
to the constitution of the body, inhaled and breathed
out in accordance with a fixed law; and this at the
moment when we utter the word becomes a voice, mani-
festing in itself the meaning (or force) of the word. In
the case of the Divine nature it has been held to be consistent with true religion that there is a Spirit (or breath)
of GOD, just as it was granted that there is also a Word
of GOD; for the Word of GOD must not be deficient as
compared with our word, which would be the case if,
while the latter was observed to be accompanied with
the emission of breath (or spirit), the former was believed
to be unaccompanied by Spirit. To suppose, however,
that some foreign element, resembling our breath, has
an influx from without into GOD, and in Him becomes
the Spirit, is a conception unworthy of GOD. On the
contrary, when we heard that there was a Word of GOD,
we did not conceive of it as something unsubstantial,
nor as finding its place in Him as the result of acquired
knowledge, nor as being uttered by the voice, and after

---

[1] ἀναγωγικῶς. The word ἀναγωγή is used by Origen to
denote the process by which we ascend from the literal to
the spiritual meaning of the Bible. Here the " ascent "
is from human nature to GOD.

[2] The same word (πνεῦμα) is used to denote both the human
breath and the Divine Spirit. It is this identity of term
which forms the starting-point of Gregory's analogy.

such utterance as passing away; nor as subject to any of the other accidents which are observed in the case of our word, but as existing after the manner of true being, possessing will and activity and omnipotence. So also, when we have learned that there is a Spirit of GOD, which accompanies the Word and manifests His activity, we do not conceive of it as an emission of breath. For the Majesty of the Divine power would be degraded, if we were to conceive of the Spirit which is in Him as like our own. But we conceive of it as a power possessing real existence in its own right and in a subsistence of its own, incapable of being separated from GOD in Whom it exists, or from the Word of GOD Whom it accompanies; not dissolving into non-existence, but like the Word of GOD, possessing an individual existence, able to will, self-moved, active, always choosing what is good, and, for the carrying out of every purpose, possessing the power corresponding to its will.

CHAPTER III

[*The Christian doctrine of GOD the mean between the doctrines of Judaism and Hellenism.*]

THE result is that he who attentively scrutinizes the depths of the mystery receives in his spirit by a secret intuition a very fair degree of apprehension of the doctrine relating to the knowledge of GOD, even though he cannot express clearly in speech the ineffable depth of this mystery, how the same thing admits of being numbered and yet escapes numeration; is perceived in a way that involves division and yet is apprehended as a unity; is distinct as regards person, and not divided as regards underlying essence.[1] For, as to person, the

¹ The word τὸ ὑποκείμενον is used by the Stoics as a synonym of οὐσία (" being," " existence "). The later Western term for this is " substance."

Spirit is one thing and the Word is another, while that to which both the Word and the Spirit belong is yet another. But when once you have grasped the distinction in these, the unity of nature again admits of no division, so that the power of the Divine sovereignty is not split up by being divided into different kinds of Godhead;[1] and, on the other hand, the statement does not coincide with the doctrine of the Jews, but the truth is a mean between the two conceptions, overthrowing each of the two schools of thought, and accepting what is useful from each. For the doctrine of the Jew is overthrown by the acceptance of the Word and by the belief in the Spirit, while the erroneous belief of the Greeks in a multiplicity of gods is effaced, since the unity of nature annuls their fancy of a plurality. And yet again, from the Jewish conception let the unity of nature remain, and from the Greek system of beliefs the distinction of persons alone, a corresponding remedy being found for the opinion entertained on either side that is inconsistent with piety. For the number of the Trinity is, as it were, a remedy for those who are in error as to the unity, while the doctrine of the unity is a remedy for those whose allegiance has been divided amongst a plurality.

CHAPTER IV

[The Jew may be convinced from Scripture of the existence of the Word and of the Spirit.]

BUT if the Jew controverts these arguments, it does not follow that our discussion with him will present equal difficulty. For the doctrines in which he has been brought up will provide the means of elucidating the truth. For the existence of a Word of GOD and Spirit

[1] Gregory is guarding against the charge of teaching " three gods."

of GOD, powers which really subsist, creating all that
has come into being, and embracing all that exists, is
most clearly shown by the inspired Scriptures. It is
sufficient to recall one piece of testimony, more ambitious
inquirers being left the task of discovering others. " By
the Word of the Lord," it is said, " the heavens were
established, and all the power of them by the breath
of His mouth." [1] By what word and what breath?
For the Word is not an utterance, and the Spirit is not
breath. For the Deity would be brought down to the
level of man after the likeness of our nature, if they were
to hold the opinion that the Maker of the universe used
a word and a breath of this kind. Moreover, what
power is there resulting from utterances and breath great
enough to suffice for the framing of the heavens and the
powers therein? For if the Word of GOD is similar to
our utterance and His Spirit similar to our breath, the
power proceeding from similar origins must certainly
be similar. But our utterances and the breath which
accompanies the utterances are inoperative and unsubstantial. Absolutely inactive and unsubstantial too will
the Divine Word and Spirit be proved to be by those
who drag down the Divine to the likeness of our word.
But if, as David says, the heavens were established by
the Word of the Lord, and the powers thereof were framed
by the Spirit of GOD, then is the mystery of the truth
established, when it instructs us to speak of a Word in
actual being and a Spirit as subsisting.

CHAPTER V

*[The creation of man and the meaning of " the image of
GOD." The origin of evil not due to the Divine will.]*

BUT it may happen that the Greek, with the help of his
general ideas, and the Jew, with his Scriptures, will not

[1] Ps. xxxiii. 6.

C

dispute the existence of a Word of GOD and a Spirit. But the design [1] of GOD the Word exhibited in His becoming man will be equally rejected by both of them as being incredible and unfit to be attributed to GOD. We shall adopt, therefore, a different starting-point in order to induce our opponents to believe in this.

Either they believe that all things were created by reason and wisdom on the part of Him Who framed the universe, or they have difficulties in admitting even this conception. But if they do not admit that reason and wisdom rule the constitution of existing things, they will set up unreason and want of skill to preside over the beginning of the universe. And if this is absurd and contrary to piety, it is plainly admitted that they will allow that reason and wisdom rule over existing things. Now we have already shown in what precedes that the Word of GOD is not this mere utterance, nor the possession of some knowledge or wisdom, but that it is a power which has a substantial existence, free to choose all that is good, and having the power to carry out all that it chooses. It has also been shown that, since the world is good, its cause is to be found in the power which produces and creates all good things. If, then, the subsistence of the whole universe depends upon the power of the Word, as the course of our argument has shown, we must on every ground conceive of no other cause of the framing of the different parts of the universe than the Word Himself, through Whom all things had their passage into being.

If any one wishes to call this either Word, or wisdom, or power, or GOD, or by any other lofty and honourable title, we will not quarrel with him. For whatever word or name is devised to denote the subject, the terms employed are indicative of one thing, the eternal power of GOD, which created existing things, which discovers

[1] Οἰκονομία is used in the Fathers to denote the " plan " of God in the Incarnation.

things that are not, which maintains created things, which foresees things to come. So then this Being, Who is GOD the Word, Wisdom, Power, has been shown in the course of our argument to be the creator of human nature, not as being impelled by some necessity to make man, but devising the production of such a creature out of superabundant love. For what was needed was that His light should not remain unseen, nor His glory without witness, nor His goodness with no one to enjoy it, and that all the other qualities, which are observed in the Divine nature, should not remain inoperative, with no one to participate in them or enjoy them.

If, then, it is for these ends that man comes into being, that he may be a partaker of the good things of GOD, of necessity he is fashioned in such a way as to fit him to participate in what is good. For as the eye by means of the bright beam planted in it by nature partakes of the light, attracting by its innate power that which is akin to it,[1] so it was necessary that with human nature there should be commingled something which was akin to the Deity, in order that by means of this corresponding gift it might have a desire for that which is nearly related to it. For even in the case of irrational creatures, whose lot it is to live in the water and in the air, each has been fashioned in a way corresponding to its mode of life, so that through the particular formation of the body each finds its own proper and kindred element, one in the air and another in the water. So then man also, who was created to enjoy the good things of GOD, needed to have in his nature something akin to that in which he was participating. For this cause he was endowed with life, reason, wisdom, and all the excellences appropriate to GOD, that by each of them he might be inspired with the desire for that which is akin to him. Since, then, one of the excellences attributed to the Divine nature is

[1] This idea is found in Plato, *Tim*. 45, B-D., and Aristotle, *de Sensu*, ii.

immortality, it was altogether necessary that the constitution of our nature should not be deprived of this too, but that it should have within it an element that is immortal, in order that through its innate capacity it might recognize that which transcended it and desire the immortality of GOD.

These truths the account of creation has indicated in a comprehensive expression by means of a single word, when it says that " man was made in the image of GOD " ; [1] for in the likeness signified by the word " image " there is contained the enumeration of all that characterizes the Divine Being, and all that Moses narrates with regard to this subject in the style of a history, setting before us doctrines in the form of narrative,[2] falls under the head of the same teaching. For that Paradise of which he speaks and the special character of the fruits, the eating of which bestows upon those who taste them, not the satisfaction of the bodily organs, but knowledge and eternity of life, all this agrees with what we have previously observed with regard to man, showing that our nature in its origin was good and surrounded by good.

But perhaps he who looks to the present condition of things objects to our statements and thinks that he can prove our description to be false, because man is not now seen to possess those blessings, but is in an entirely contrary state. For where is the Divine likeness in the soul? Where is the freedom of the body from the passions? Where is the eternity of life? Man is a fleeting being, subject to passions, a prey to mortality, exposed to every form of suffering in body and soul. By these and the like statements and by inveighing against our nature, he will think that he disproves the account which we have given of man. But in order that our discourse may not be diverted at any point from its proper sequence, we will briefly discuss these objections.

[1] Gen. i. 27.
[2] With this passage cp. Origen, *de Princ.*, iv. 6.

The fact that human life is at present in an abnormal condition is no adequate proof that man never was in possession of what is good. For since man is the work of GOD, who out of goodness brought this creature into existence, it cannot reasonably be suspected that he, whose constitution has its origin in goodness, was created by his Maker in a state of evil; whereas the fact that we are now in this condition and that we have been deprived of a more desirable estate is due to a different cause. Here, again, the principle which forms the starting-point for our argument is one which does not lie outside the assent of our opponents. For He Who made man that he might participate in His own peculiar blessings, and established in his nature the means of acquiring all forms of excellence, in order that through each endowment his desire might be borne on by a corresponding movement towards its like, would not have deprived him of the noblest and most precious of blessings, I mean the gift of independence and free-will. For if some necessity had directed human life, the image would have been falsified in that respect, becoming alien by its unlikeness to its archetype. For how could that nature which is under the yoke and bondage of certain necessities be called an image of the sovereign nature? Accordingly that which in every respect has been made to resemble the Deity must assuredly possess in its nature self-determination and independence, so that the participation in good may be the reward of virtue.

Whence comes it, then, you will say, that he who was honoured with the most noble endowments exchanged these blessings for a worse condition? That, too, admits of clear explanation. The production of evil in no case had its origin in the Divine will. For vice would be free from blame if it could claim GOD as its creator and father. But evil springs up in some way from within, arising in the will whenever there is any withdrawal of the soul from what is excellent. For as sight is an activity of nature, and blindness is the privation of this natural activity, so virtue is opposed to vice. For we cannot conceive of vice as originating in any other way than as the absence of virtue.[1] For as when light is withdrawn darkness supervenes, but when light is present it does not exist, so, as long as good is present in the nature, vice has no independent existence of its own, while the withdrawal of the better element brings into existence its opposite. Since, then, it is the characteristic of freewill to choose freely that which pleases it, it is not GOD Who is the cause of your present ills, seeing that He constituted your nature in a state of independence and freedom, but man's folly in preferring the worse instead of the better.

CHAPTER VI

[Evil a disturbance of the divinely ordered harmony of the intelligent and sensible elements in man. Of the envy of the devil and how he beguiled man to turn away from GOD.]

BUT perchance you may ask the cause of this error of judgment. For to this point logical sequence leads our argument. Here again, then, some principle will be found in accordance with reason, which will elucidate this question. The traditional account which we have received from the Fathers is somewhat as follows. This teaching is not a mythical account, but draws its power of winning conviction from our nature itself.

A twofold classification may be observed in existing things, our observation of them being divided between the world of intelligence and the world of sense. And besides these nothing can be perceived in the nature of existing things which falls outside this division. And these are separated from one another by a considerable

[1] See Introduction, p. 13.

interval, so that the sensible nature does not exhibit the characteristics of the intelligible nature, nor the intelligible those of the sensible, but each of them receives its particular character from qualities opposite to those of the other. For the intelligible nature is something incorporeal, impalpable, and formless, but the sensible, as its very name implies, falls within the apprehension of the senses. But just as in the sensible world itself, in spite of the great contrariety of its elements, a certain harmony has been devised by the wisdom which presides over the universe, a harmony effected by means of opposites, and so there is effected an inner harmony of all creation, the chain of agreement being nowhere broken by the natural contrariety ; in the same way there is also, as a result of the Divine wisdom, a mixture and blending of the sensible and the intelligible, in order that everything may equally participate in the good, and none of the things which exist may be excluded from a share in the nature of that which is superior. Therefore though the proper sphere for the intelligible nature is the realm of subtle and mobile essence, having by virtue of its dwelling above the universe considerable affinity with the intelligible element in accordance with the peculiarity of its nature, yet by virtue of a higher wisdom there is a certain commingling of the intelligible world with the sensible creation, so that no part of creation might be rejected, as the Apostle says,[1] nor deprived of Divine fellowship.

On this account the blending of the intelligible and the sensible elements which we find in man is exhibited by the Divine nature, as the account of creation teaches. For GOD, it says, taking dust [2] from the earth fashioned man and by His own breath planted life in the creature which He formed, in order that the earthly element might be raised by union with the Divine, and so the Divine grace in one even course, as it were, might uni-

<hr />

[1] 1 Tim. iv. 4. [2] Gen. ii. 7.

formly extend through all creation, the lower nature being mingled with that which is above the world.

When the intelligible creation was already in existence, and the Power which rules the universe had assigned to each of the angelic powers [1] a certain activity in the constitution of the universe, there was a certain power also which was appointed to maintain and govern the region about the earth, equipped for this very task by the Power which governs the universe. Then there was fashioned that figure moulded of earth, a representation of the supreme Power. This living creature was man. In him there was the godlike beauty of the intelligible nature, blended with a certain ineffable potency. That is why he to whom was assigned the government of the world takes it amiss, and finds it intolerable, that out of the nature subject to him there should be manifested any being resembling the supreme dignity.

But how it was that he who had been created for no evil end by Him Who framed the universe in goodness fell away into the passion of envy, it is no part of the present treatise to discuss in detail, but we may briefly offer the explanation of it to those who are inclined to listen. For the distinction of virtue and vice is not conceived of as a distinction of two things which appear as actually existing. But just as the non-existent is logically opposed to that which exists, and it is not possible to say that the non-existent is distinguished from that which exists, so far as actual subsistence is concerned, but we say that non-existence is logically opposed to existence; in the same way, also, vice is opposed to virtue, not as having an existence of its own, but because it is conceived of as arising from the absence of the good. And just as we say that blindness is logically opposed to sight, not because blindness naturally has an existence

[1] This idea is found in Origen. It may be a reminiscence of the *Timaeus* of Plato, though later Judaism exhibits parallel teaching.

of its own, but because it is the privation of a former possession, so also we say that vice is found where there is a privation of good, just as a shadow follows upon the withdrawal of the sun's ray.

Since, then, the uncreated nature does not admit of movement in the direction of change or alteration or variation, whereas everything which came into being through an act of creation has a natural tendency to change, because the very subsistence of creation owed its beginning to change, the non-existent passing by a change into existence through the Divine power; since, too, the power which we have already mentioned was also created, and chose by a movement of his own will whatever he thought fit, after he had closed his eyes to what was good and free from envy, just as he who in the sunlight covers his eyes with his eyelids and sees darkness, so he, too, by the very fact that he would not perceive the good, learned to know that which was contrary to good. And that is envy.[1]

Now it is admitted that the first cause of anything is responsible for all that follows in due sequence upon it, as for example upon health there follows a good bodily condition, activity, an enjoyable life; whereas on disease there follows weakness, inactivity, a life of discomfort. So also in everything else the results follow in natural sequence their own proper causes. As then freedom from passion is the beginning and foundation of the life of virtue, so the inclination to vice which arose through envy proved the road to all the evils which have been shown to follow it. For when once he, who by turning away from good begat envy within himself, came to possess this inclination to evil, like a rock, which breaking away from the ridge of a mountain is carried headlong by its own weight, so he too, torn away from his natural affinity to good, and inclining towards vice, by his own movement, as it were by a weight, was forced

[1] Cp. Wisdom ii. 23, 24.

along and carried to the uttermost bound of wickedness; and that faculty of mind which he received from the Creator to help him in sharing in good, he employed to assist him in discovering evil devices, and by his deceit cleverly overreaches man and persuades him to become his own murderer and assassin.

In virtue of the power which man had received through the Divine blessing, he possessed an exalted rank. For he was appointed to rule over the earth and all that was on it. He was beauteous in form, for he had been created as a representation of the archetypal beauty. His nature was free from passion, for he was a copy of Him Who is passionless. He was frank and open, revelling in the Divine Presence even face to face. All this served to incite in his adversary the passion of envy.

But he was unable to work his will by any display of strength or violent exercise of power, for the power of God's blessing prevailed over his violence. Therefore he plots how he may detach him from the power which gave him his strength, in order that he may be made an easy prey to his plotting. And as in the case of a lamp, when the flame has caught the wick, if any one, being unable to blow out the flame, mixes water with the oil, he will by this device render the flame dull, so the adversary, by fraudulently mingling vice with man's will, succeeded in extinguishing, in a way, and obscuring the Divine blessing; and when this failed, its opposite of necessity entered in. Now the opposite of life is death, of power weakness, of the blessing the curse, of frankness shame, and of all good things those which are conceived as opposed to them. That is why humanity is in its present evil state; for that beginning provided the means of reaching such an end.

CHAPTER VII

[Why did GOD create man if He foresaw the evils resulting from his fall ? First answer. Moral evil is not due to GOD, but to man's self-will in turning away from GOD.]

LET no one ask whether GOD foresaw the calamity which would befall man as a result of his folly, when He came to create him, since it would have been more profitable for him never to have come into being than to exist in such evil case. For these objections are urged by those who have been deceived and led away by the doctrines of the Manichees in order to establish their own error, by way of showing thus that the Creator of man's nature is evil.[1] For if GOD is ignorant of none of the things which exist, and yet man is in a state of evil, we can no longer preserve intact the doctrine of GOD's goodness, if he brought into life man, who was destined to live in a state of evil. For if activity in good is always the characteristic of a nature which is good, this life of sorrow and mortality can no longer, it is maintained, be referred to the workmanship of Him Who is good, but we must suppose that such a life springs from a different cause, whose nature is inclined to evil.

All these and the like arguments for those who are deeply tinged with the deceit of heresy, as with some indelible dye, seem to derive a certain force from their superficial plausibility, but those who have a clearer perception of the truth plainly see that they are in-effective and afford a ready proof of their fallacious character. I think, too, that it is right to put forward

[1] The Manichæans taught that there were two ultimate principles, light and darkness. The first human beings were regarded as the offspring of evil powers. See article " Manichæism " in Hasting's *Encyclopædia of Religion and Ethics.*

the Apostle in support of our condemnation of them. For in his discourse to the Corinthians [1] he distinguishes between the carnal and the spiritual conditions of souls, showing, as I think, by what he says that it is not fitting to judge good or evil by the perception of the senses, but that we ought to withdraw the intelligence from bodily phenomena and distinguish the nature of good and its opposite as it is in itself. For, says he, " the spiritual man judgeth of all things."

The cause of the fabrication of these fabulous doctrines in the case of those who put forward such views, is, I think, this, that in their definition of good they look to the pleasure of bodily enjoyment, and because the nature of the body, being composite and tending to dissolution, is necessarily subject to vicissitudes and ailments, and there follows on such sufferings a certain sensation of pain, they think that the creation of man is the work of an evil GOD. Since, if their thought had turned its gaze in a higher direction, and if, diverting the intelligence from the state induced by pleasures, they had considered, free from passion, the nature of existing things, they would have come to think that nothing is evil except wickedness. All wickedness finds its characteristic in the privation of good, seeing that it has no existence of its own and is not found to possess any substantial being; for nothing that is evil lies outside the will or is independent of it, but it derives its name from the non-existence of the good. That which is not has no real existence, and the Creator of really existent things is not the Creator of that which possesses no real existence.

Hence GOD, Who is the author of that which is, not of that which is not, has no responsibility for what is evil; seeing that He made sight, not blindness; He manifested virtue, not the privation of virtue; He proposed as the prize in the struggle of free-will, for those who live their

[1] I Cor. ii. 14–15.

lives in accordance with virtue, the privilege of enjoying all good things ; nor did he subject human nature to some forcible compulsion to do His pleasure, drawing it towards good against its will, as though it were some lifeless vessel. But if any one, when the light shines brightly from a clear sky, of his own free will covers his eyes with his eyelids, he cannot blame the sun for his failure to see it.

CHAPTER VIII

[Second answer to the objection stated in the previous chapter. GOD provided against the effects of man's fall. It was better to restore man by repentance and suffering than never to have created him at all. The restoration of man was a task worthy of GOD.]

YET he who has in view the dissolution of the body in any case feels indignant and counts it a hardship that our life suffers dissolution in death, and asserts that this is the extremity of ill, that our outward life should suffer extinction through this state of mortality. Let him consider, then, the exceeding greatness of the Divine beneficence manifested through this dismal necessity, for perhaps by this he may be all the more induced to wonder at the graciousness of GOD's care for man. Those who participate in life find life desirable for the sake of enjoying what is acceptable to them. For if a man should pass his whole life in pain, such an one judges it far preferable not to exist than to exist in a state of suffering. Let us then inquire whether He Who gave us life has any other aim than that we should live under the fairest conditions.

For since by a movement of the will we acquired fellowship with evil, by some indulgence in pleasure mingling evil with our nature, like a deadly poison sweetened with honey, and so by falling from the blessedness which the mind associates with freedom from passion, we became transformed to evil, therefore, like an earthen vessel, man is again resolved into earth, in order that the foulness which is now included in his nature may be sifted out, and he may be refashioned by the resurrection in his original form.

Some such doctrine Moses [1] sets before us after the manner of a history and in allegories. Yet the teaching which these allegories contain is clear. For since, as he says, the first human beings became involved in what was forbidden and were stripped naked of that state of blessedness, the Lord clothes these first-formed creatures with coats of skin. He does not, I think, intend to apply the sense of the word to these literal skins. For what kind of animals were they, which, when slain and flayed, supplied the covering which was devised for them? But since every skin when separated from the animal is a dead thing, I certainly think that He Who heals our wickedness in His forethought subsequently clothed men with that capacity for dying, which was the special characteristic of the irrational nature, though not with the view of its lasting for ever. For a coat is one of those things which are put on as from without, offering to the body its use for a time, but not a part of its natural equipment.

The nature, therefore, which was created for immortality was invested by way of accommodation with the garment of mortality derived from the nature of irrational creatures, and enfolding the outward, not the inward, part of man, embracing the sentient part of his nature, but not laying hold of the Divine image itself.[2] Now

[1] Gen. iii. 21.

[2] The allegorical interpretation of the " coats of skin " is found in Clement of Alexandria and Origen, and finds a parallel in the Gnostics and in Rabbinic writings. But in Origen the coats of skin denote the body with which man was clothed after the Fall, whereas in Gregory they denote the condition of mortality. This latter interpretation is also that of Methodius.

the sentient part suffers dissolution, but is not destroyed. For destruction is the passing into non-existence, but dissolution is the diffusion again into the constituent elements of the universe, from which it was formed. Now that which is in this condition has not perished, even though it escapes the apprehension of our senses.

The cause of dissolution is made plain by the illustration we have given. For since the perception of the senses is closely related to the gross and earthly element, while the nature of the intelligence is superior to, and higher than, the motions of sense, the result is that, as it was by the arbitrament of the senses that man's judgment of the good went astray, while deviation from the good brought into existence the contrary state of things, that part of us, which was rendered useless by receiving the contrary element, suffers dissolution. Our illustration may be put as follows.[1] Let us suppose a vessel to have been formed out of clay, and that this has been filled with molten lead by some act of treachery, and that the lead when poured in becomes hard and remains there, so that it cannot be poured out. Suppose, too, that the owner lays claim to the vessel, and, since he is skilled in the potter's craft, he pounds into pieces the earthenware about the lead, and in this way subsequently remodels the vessel in its former shape for his own use, after it has been emptied of the material which had been mingled with it. In like manner then He Who fashioned our vessel, after vice has been mingled with the sentient part of it, I mean the bodily part, by dissolving the material which had received the evil, and again remoulding it free from the contrary element by the resurrection, will fashion it afresh in its original beauty.

Now there is a kind of bond and fellowship in the sinful passions between soul and body, and there is a certain analogy between the death of the body and that

[1] The illustration here given is found in Methodius, *de Resurr.*, i. 44. See Introduction, p. 14.

of the soul. For as in the case of the flesh we call separation from sentient life death, so also in the case of the
soul we give the name of death to the separation from
true life. We observe, then, as we have said, one and
the same participation in evil on the part of both soul
and body, for through both of them wickedness comes
into active play. The death which consists in the dissolution resulting from the clothing with dead skins does
not indeed touch the soul. For how can that be dis-
solved which is not composite? But since there was a
need that its stains too, contracted through sin, should
be removed by some remedy, the medicine of virtue was
applied to it in the present life, in order to heal such
wounds. But if it remains unhealed, its cure has been
provided for in the life which follows hereafter.[1]

But just as in the body there are different kinds of
ailments, some of which admit of being cured more
easily, others with greater difficulty, and in these latter
applications of the knife, caustics, and bitter draughts
of medicine are resorted to in order to remove the affection which has seized the body, so the judgment which
follows hereafter announces to us something of the same
sort for the cure of the ailments of the soul. To the
more thoughtless it is a threat and a stern method of
correction, in order that through fear of a painful retribution we may be brought to our senses and led to flee
from wickedness, while the more discerning believe it to
be a process of healing and a cure provided by GOD by
way of restoring His own creature, whom He formed, to
his original grace. For as they who remove by the knife
or caustics the moles and warts, which have been formed

[1] The language of the whole of this passage is strongly
coloured with Platonism. Gregory seems in this passage to
teach a purely moral improvement to be followed by a
purification of the soul hereafter, without reference to the
Christian doctrine of redemption which he deals with in
later chapters. For his teaching on the purification of souls
see Chap. XXXV, and Introduction, p. 13 f.

upon the body contrary to nature, do not apply to him whom they are relieving a method of healing that is free from pain, so, too, whatever material excrescences become encrusted upon our souls, when they have become carnal through participation in the body's passions, are cut away and removed by that ineffable wisdom and power of Him Who, as the Gospel says, healeth the wicked. For, as He says, "they that are whole need not a physician, but they that are sick." [1]

The close affinity which has been established between the soul and evil has the following result. The excision of a wart gives a sharp sensation to the surface of the body. For an unnatural growth upon the nature affects the subject by a kind of sympathy, and there is a certain unexpected commingling of the foreign element with our own being, so that our feelings experience a painful and stinging sensation when separated from the element which is contrary to nature. In like manner when the soul pines and is wasted away in the reproaches incurred for sin, as prophecy somewhere says,[2] owing to its deeply rooted connexion with evil, there follow of necessity certain inexpressible and indescribable pains, which defy description no less than does the nature of the good things which we hope for. For neither the one nor the other can be expressed in words or conjectured by the mind.

Any one, therefore, who looks to the aim proposed by the wisdom of Him Who governs the universe will not on any reasonable ground be so short-sighted as to call the Creator of men the author of evil, saying that either He is ignorant of the future, or that, if He knew it and still created man, He is not free from the impulse towards evil. For He knew what would happen, and yet did not check the impulse which led to that which came to pass. For

[1] Luke v. 31 (cp. Mark ii. 17; Matt. ix. 12).
[2] Ps. xxxviii. (xxxix.) 12 in the Greek Bible (xxxix. 11, Eng. Vers.).

D

the fact that humanity would desert the path of goodness was not unknown to Him Who embraces all things by His faculty of knowledge, and sees the future equally with the past. But as He contemplated man's perversion, so also He perceived his recall to what is good. Which, then, was the better course, not to have brought our nature into existence at all, since He foresaw that he who would come into being would fall short of good, or, when He had brought him into being, to recall him by repentance, even when in a state of disease, to his original grace?

But to call GOD the creator of evil because of the bodily pains which of necessity result from the unstable character of man's nature or to imagine that He is in no way the creator of man, so as to avoid conceiving of Him as the author of those experiences which give us pain, is a proof of the extreme short-sightedness of those who distinguish good and evil by the senses, and who do not know that that alone is in its own nature good, which is not embraced by sense-perception, and that that alone is evil which consists in alienation from the true good. To make pains and pleasures the criterion of good and its opposite is a characteristic of the irrational nature, seeing that in such beings the power to perceive what is truly good has no place, as they are destitute of mind and understanding. But from what we have already said it is clear that man is GOD's work, created good and for good ends, and it may be proved by countless other arguments, the greater number of which we shall pass over, because they are endless.

When we call GOD the creator of man we have not forgotten the points which we carefully defined in the prelude of our argument against the Greeks, in which it was shown [1] that the Word of GOD is a substantial and personal being and is both GOD and Word, embracing in Himself all creative power, or rather He is in Himself power, and possesses the impulse to all good, and in effect-

[1] See Chap. I.

ing all that He wills He has a power corresponding to His purpose. His will and work is the life of existing things; by Him man was introduced into life, adorned after the Divine likeness with the noblest gifts.

Now that alone is unchangeable in its nature which does not come into being through creation, whereas whatever the uncreated nature has brought into being out of a state of non-existence, as soon as it has begun to exist as the result of a transformation, is continually passing through a state of change; such change, if the creature acts in accordance with nature, being always in the better direction, whereas, if it is perverted from the right path, a movement in the opposite direction awaits it.

Such was the state of man, the changeable part of whose nature had lapsed in the contrary direction. And when once the withdrawal from good had taken place, its consequence was the introduction of every form of evil, so that as a result of the withdrawal of life death was introduced instead; on the privation of light there followed darkness; and in the absence of virtue wickedness took its place, and for every kind of good there was substituted the list of opposite evils. When man had fallen into these evils and the like as a result of his folly (for it was impossible that he should possess prudence, who had turned away from prudence; or form any wise decision, who had departed from wisdom), by whom was he to be recalled to his original grace? To whom did it belong to raise up the fallen, to recall the lost, to lead by the hand him who had gone astray? To whom else but to Him Who is absolutely Lord of his nature? For to Him alone Who originally gave him life was it possible and fitting to recall it when it was lost. This is what we are taught by the revelation of the truth, when we learn that GOD created man originally and saved him when he had fallen.

CHAPTER IX

[The objection urged against the Incarnation that it involved a degradation of the Divine nature. Gregory replies that only moral evil brings degradation, whereas the Incarnation was a display of moral perfection.]

BUT thus far our argument will, perhaps, obtain the assent of him who considers its logical sequence, because nothing that we have said seems to lie outside a worthy conception of GOD.   But he will not think the same with regard to what follows, the facts in which the revelation of the truth receives its strongest confirmation, the human birth and the growth from infancy to full manhood, the eating and drinking, the weariness and sleep, the grief and tears, the false charges and the tribunal of judgment, the Cross, the death, the placing in the tomb.   For all these facts, comprised as they are in the revelation, blunt in a way the faith of little minds, so that they do not accept the rest of our argument on account of what precedes.   For they do not admit what is worthy of GOD in the resurrection from the dead, because of that which is unworthy of Him in the death.

Our first duty, I think, is to divert our thoughts from the grossness of the flesh, and contemplate the good in itself, as well as its opposite, and the distinctive features by which we apprehend each of them.   For I suppose that no one who has carefully pondered the matter will deny that one thing alone in the whole universe is disgraceful by nature, and that is the weakness which attaches to moral evil, whereas that which is free from moral evil is devoid of disgrace; and that with which nothing shameful is mingled is beyond all doubt recognized as included in the good; while that which is truly good has no mixture of the contrary.   Now everything which is seen to be included in the category of good is consistent with GOD's character. Either, then, let them show that birth, nurture, growth, advancement towards the maturity of nature, the experience of death, the return from death, constitute moral evil, or, if they agree that the experiences just mentioned fall outside the scope of evil, they will of necessity admit that there is nothing disgraceful in what is free from moral evil. And since that which is free from all disgrace and moral evil is plainly shown to be good, how are they not to be pitied for their folly who maintain the view that that which is good is not befitting in the case of GOD?

CHAPTER X

[*Second objection to the Incarnation, " How can the finite contain the infinite ? " Gregory replies by the analogy of the soul in man and the illustration of the flame and the wick.*]

" BUT," it is said, " human nature is an insignificant and circumscribed thing, and how could the infinite have been contained in the atom ? " But who maintains that the infinity of the Godhead was contained in the circumscribed limits of the flesh, as in a kind of vessel? For not even in our own life is the faculty of thought enclosed within the limits of the flesh. But while the bulk of the body is limited by its own particular parts, the soul in the movements of its thought ranges at will [1] over the whole creation ; it ascends to heaven, it sets its foot within the deep, it traverses the wide expanse of the world ; in its unwearying activity it penetrates to the underworld, and is often engaged in comprehending the wonders of the heavens, in no degree burdened by the appendage of the body.

If the soul of man, though commingled with the body

---

[1] Gregory is perhaps thinking of the similar passage in Plato, *Phaedrus*, 246, B.

by the law of its nature, ranges everywhere at will, what
need is there to say that the Godhead is circumscribed by
the limits of the fleshly nature, and why may we not rather,
with the help of illustrations which we can understand,
form some conjecture worthy of the subject, with regard
to GOD's plan in the Incarnation?   For as in the case of
a lamp we see the flame laying hold of the material
supplied to it, and reason distinguishes between the flame
attached to the material and the material which kindles
the flame, though actually it is not possible to separate
them from one another and show the flame separate and
distinct from the material, but both together form a
unity, so also is it in the present case.   Let no one, I pray,
associate with this illustration the perishable character
of the flame, but let him accept only whatever is suitable
in the simile, and reject what is inconsistent.   In the same
way, then, as we see the flame clinging to that which is
supplied to it, and not included in the material, what is
there to prevent us from apprehending a kind of union and
approximation of a nature which is divine to humanity,
and preserving even in this approximation a right and
proper conception of GOD, while retaining our belief that
the Divine Being is free from all circumscription, even
though He be in man?

CHAPTER XI

*[The union of the Divine and human natures in Christ is
    as inscrutable as the union of soul and body in man.
    But the fact, as distinct from the manner, is shown by
    the miracles which Christ worked.]*

IF you ask how the Godhead blends itself with humanity,
it is time for you first to ask what is the character of the
union between the flesh and the soul.   If you are ignorant
of the manner in which your soul is united to the body,
you certainly must not suppose that that previous question

either ought to come within the range of your apprehension. On the contrary, as in our own case we have come to believe that the soul is something distinct from the body, because the flesh when deprived of the soul becomes dead and inoperative, and yet we know not the manner of their union, so also in the former case we acknowledge that the Divine nature differs from this mortal and perishable nature, as possessing greater majesty than it, but the way in which the Divine Being blends Himself with man we are not capable of perceiving.

The fact that GOD came in man's nature the miracles which are recorded prevent us from doubting, but the manner in which it was brought about we decline to investigate, as being beyond the reach of processes of reasoning. For though we believe that the whole corporeal and intelligent creation derived its being from the incorporeal and uncreated nature, we do not combine with our faith in these truths an investigation of the source or the manner. On the contrary, accepting the fact that it was created, we put aside all curious inquiry into the manner in which the universe was framed, as being altogether beyond description and inexpressible.

CHAPTER XII

[The Incarnation is attested by the signs of Divine power shown in the life of Christ, which are parallel to the wonders of GOD in Creation.

LET him who seeks for proofs of the fact that GOD has been manifested to us in the flesh consider His activities. For of the existence of GOD at all there can be no other proof than the testimony supplied by His very activities. As then by looking at the universe and examining the orderly dispositions exhibited in the world and the displays of beneficence which GOD effects in our life we apprehend the existence of a transcendent Power, which created all that comes into being and preserves all that exists, so also in the case of GOD manifested to us by means of the flesh we regard as a sufficient proof of the manifestation of the Godhead the wonders displayed in His activities, marking by means of His recorded works all the characteristic qualities of the Divine Nature.

To GOD it belongs to give life to men, to GOD to preserve by His providence all that exists, to GOD to bestow food and drink on those who have been granted life in the flesh, to GOD to benefit the needy, to GOD to restore to itself again by means of health the nature which had been perverted by sickness, to GOD to rule over equally the whole creation, earth, sea, air, and the regions above the air, to GOD to possess power sufficient for every need, and above all to show mastery over death and corruption. If, then, in any of these and the like prerogatives the narrative concerning Him had been defective, those who are strangers to the faith would have had good reason to take exception to our religion; whereas if all the characteristics which enable us to conceive of GOD are clearly perceived in the narratives about Him, what is there to prove an obstacle to faith?

CHAPTER XIII

[The circumstances of Christ's birth and death, while they show that He was subject to the conditions of our nature, also show that He transcended them.]

BUT, it is said, birth and death are a characteristic of the fleshly nature. I agree. But that which precedes the birth and that which follows the death transcend the common experience of our nature. For by looking to either limit of human life, we know both the source from which we take our beginning and what is the end where we cease to be. For as man begins his existence as the result of a weakness, so by a weakness does he attain his end. But in that other case neither did the birth begin in a weakness, nor did the death end in weakness. For neither was His birth preceded by pleasure, nor was His death succeeded by corruption.

Do you disbelieve the miracle? I am delighted at your disbelief, for, by the very reasons which lead you to consider that the account surpasses belief, you admit that these wonderful events are above nature. Let this very fact, then, that the Gospel message does not proceed in a way that accords with nature, be a proof to you of the Deity of Him Who was manifested. For if the narratives about Christ had kept within the limits of nature, where were the Divine Being? But if the account surpasses nature, the very facts which occasion your disbelief constitute a proof that He Whom we preach is GOD.

For man is begotten by the intercourse of two persons, and after death he passes into a state of corruption. If the Gospel message had contained these features, you certainly would not have considered Him to be GOD of Whom it is testified that He shared in the conditions proper to our nature. But when you hear that He came into existence, but that He surpassed the common lot of our nature both in the manner of His birth and in the fact that He was incapable of the change into corruption, you would do well if, consistently with these facts, you exhibited incredulity in the other direction, and refused to think of Him as an ordinary man like those produced in the course of nature.

For he who does not believe that such an one is man, must of necessity be led on to believe Him to be GOD. For he who recorded that He was born, at the same time narrated also that He was born of a virgin. If, then, it is credible, in virtue of what is told us, that He was born, on the strength of this same evidence it is by no means incredible that He was born in this particular manner. For he who spoke of the birth added also that He was born of a virgin; and he who made mention of His death testified to His resurrection as well as to the death. If, then, as a result of what you hear, you admit that He both died and was born, on the same grounds you will certainly admit that both His birth and His death were free from weakness. Yet these facts transcend nature. Hence He Who is shown to have appeared in conditions which surpass nature certainly does not fall within the order of nature.

CHAPTER XIV

[Why did GOD submit to the humiliation of becoming man ?

WHAT, then, is the reason, it is urged, why the Divine Being descended to this low estate, so that faith wavers at the thought that GOD, the infinite, incomprehensible, ineffable reality, which is above all glory and majesty, should mingle with the defilement of human nature, so that His sublime activities also should be degraded by association with that which is base ?

CHAPTER XV

[The cause of the Incarnation was GOD'S love for man. Further objection, " Why did not GOD restore man by a mere decree ? " Gregory does not fully answer this till Chapter XVII, but asserts meanwhile that there was nothing unworthy of GOD in the method which He chose.]

To this question also we have no difficulty in finding an answer which accords with our conception of GOD. Do you ask the reason why GOD was born amongst men? If you take out of life the various benefits bestowed on us by GOD, you will not be able to say what means you have of recognizing the Divine. For it is by the blessings we enjoy that we recognize our benefactor, seeing that we look at the things which befall us, and from them we infer the nature of Him Who occasions them. If, then, love towards man is a special feature of the Divine nature, you have the explanation for which you asked; you have the reason for the presence of GOD among men.

For our nature, being weak, needed a healer; man who had fallen needed some one to raise him up; he who had lost life needed a life-giver; he who had fallen away from the participation in good needed some one to restore him to good; he who was shut up in darkness needed the presence of the light; the captive sought some one to ransom him; he who was bound sought some one to help him; he who was held in the yoke of slavery sought some one to set him free. Were these slight and unworthy reasons to importune GOD to " come down " to " visit " [1] human nature, seeing that humanity was in so pitiable and wretched a condition?

" But," it is urged, " it was possible for man to be benefited, and at the same time for GOD to remain free from weakness and suffering. For why did not He, Who framed the universe by His will and called into being that which was not, wrest man by an immediate and divine act of authority [2] from the hostile power, and restore him to his original condition, if that were His pleasure? Whereas He traverses long and circuitous routes, submits to a bodily nature, enters into human life by means of birth, and passing through each age in turn, He afterwards ' tastes of death,' [3] and so by the resurrection of His own body accomplishes His aim, as though it were not in His power to remain in the height of His Divine glory and save man by a command, leaving on one side such circuitous ways? " In the face, then, of objections of this kind we must set out the truth, that no obstacle may be

[1] Cp. Ex. iii. 8; iv. 31.
[2] A similar objection is dealt with by Athanasius, *de Incarnatione*, 44.
[3] Heb. ii. 9.

put in the way of the faith of those who seek by exact inquiry the rational ground of the Christian revelation.

In the first place, then, let us consider, as we have already in what precedes inquired to some extent,[1] what is the direct opposite of virtue. As darkness is the opposite of light, and death of life, so vice, and nothing else but vice, it is clear, is the opposite of virtue. For just as there are many things in creation, but none of them is distinguished by way of opposition to light or life, not stone, or wood, or water, or man, or any other existing thing, save only those things which are conceived of as their exact opposites, such as darkness and death, so also in the case of virtue it will not be maintained that any created thing is conceived of as its opposite, except the idea of vice.

If, then, our teaching had maintained that the Divine Being came into a state of vice, the opponent would have had a good chance of inveighing against our faith, on the ground that we hold doctrines about the Divine nature which are absurd and incongruous. For indeed it would have been impious to assert that He Who is very wisdom and goodness and incorruption, and Who possesses every other exalted quality that is conceived of or named, should change to the opposite. If, then, GOD is truly and essentially virtue, and no existing thing of any kind is logically opposed to virtue, but only vice, and GOD is not found in a state of vice, but in the nature of man; since, further, the only thing which is unseemly and disgraceful is the weakness of vice, which GOD neither has experienced, nor does His nature permit Him to experience, why are they ashamed of the confession that GOD assumed human nature, seeing that in the constitution of man there is nothing which is contradictory to the idea of virtue? For neither rational thought, nor the faculty of understanding, nor the capacity for exact knowledge, nor any other faculty, which is peculiar to man's being, is opposed to the conception of virtue.

[1] See Chaps. V–VIII.

CHAPTER XVI

[Further objection. " The change involved in human birth exposed GOD to weakness." Gregory distinguishes between two senses of the word " weakness " ($\pi \acute{a} \theta o s$). The weakness involved in the Incarnation was physical, not moral, and its issue was a new principle of life for man through Christ's resurrection.]

" BUT," it is maintained, " the very change [1] experienced by our body is a weakness.[2] He who is born in this condition is born in weakness; whereas the Divine Being is free from all weakness. It is, then, a conception foreign to GOD which men form if they declare that He Who is exempt from all weakness came to share a state of weakness." But in reply to this objection we shall use the same argument, that the word " weakness " is used sometimes in a proper sense, and sometimes with an extension of meaning.[3] Now that which lays hold of the will and perverts it from virtue to vice is truly a weakness, whereas

[1] Gregory is referring to the mutability which characterizes all created things as contrasted with the unchanging life of GOD.

[2] The word $\pi \acute{a} \theta o s$, here translated " weakness," has several distinct senses, which no one English word adequately covers. Gregory here distinguishes between what he calls the " proper " sense of the term, in which it used to denote any form of moral " weakness," and the " extended " sense of the term in which it is applied to the changes and vicissitudes involved in the natural processes of human life, *e. g.* birth and death. In the former sense the Incarnation did not, he urges, involve any contact with moral evil. In the latter sense, the birth and death of Christ did not involve the Divine Being in subjection to the vicissitudes of human life any more than the physician is involved in the ailments of his patients.

[3] The word $\kappa \alpha \tau \acute{a} \chi \rho \eta \sigma \iota s$ is used like the Latin word *abusio* in Quintilian (*Inst.*, viii. 2, 5; cp. 6, 34) to denote an extension or adaptation of words to meet the defects of language. I owe these references to Mr. F. H. Colson.

everything that successively occurs in nature, as it proceeds in its own proper sequence, would more properly be called a form of activity rather than a weakness, such as birth, growth, the permanence of the subject through the influx and efflux of nourishment, the combination of the constituent elements of the body, and, on the other hand, the dissolution of that which has been brought together and its return into the kindred elements.

What, then, is it which our religion asserts that the Divine Being assumed? Is it that which is properly called "a weakness," that is vice, or is it that which is a natural movement? For if our teaching had maintained that the Divine Being was involved in what is forbidden, then it would have been necessary to shun such a perverse belief, seeing that its teaching with regard to the Divine nature was absolutely unsound. But if it maintains that He laid hold of our nature, the creation of which, in the first place, and its subsistence, originated in Him, in what point does our preaching fall short of a conception which is worthy of GOD, seeing that into the notions we form of GOD no state induced by weakness enters along with our belief? For we do not say that the physician incurs weakness when he heals him who is subject to weakness; but even though he comes into contact with the ailment, the healer remains untouched by the weakness.

If birth in itself is not a weakness, neither will life be called a weakness. But human birth is preceded by the passion of sensual pleasure, and the impulse to vice in living beings is an ailment of our nature. Yet our religion teaches that He was pure from both these. If, then, His birth was unattended by sensual pleasure, and His life by vice, what weakness is left, which the mystery of godliness asserts GOD to have shared?

If the objector calls the severance of body and soul a weakness, he would be much more justified in so naming the combination of them both. For if the separation of elements which have been connected is a weakness, the conjunction of elements which have been separate will be a weakness too. For there is a change of a sort in the combination of elements that have been apart as well as in the severance of elements that have been conjoined or united.

The name, then, which we give to the last change ought properly to be applied to the preceding change also. If the first change, which we call birth, is not a weakness, neither can the second change, that which we call death, by which the combination of soul and body is severed, be termed with any show of reason a weakness.

Now we say that GOD experienced each of these two changes of our nature, both that through which the soul is united with the body, and that by which the body is separated from the soul; and we affirm that, mingling with each of these elements, I mean the sensible and the intelligent elements in the composition of man, by means of that ineffable and inexpressible combination he carried out this design, that the union of the elements, when once they had been united, should remain for ever.

For when our nature, in His case also, had in its own proper course undergone the change which results in the separation of the body and the soul, He again united the severed elements by a kind of cement, as it were, by which I mean the Divine power, recombining that which was severed in a union which could not be broken. And this is the resurrection, the return, after dissolution, of elements which had been united to a union which is indissoluble, so that they are knit together; in order that the primal grace associated with human nature might be recalled, and we might return once more to eternal life, when once the vice mingled with our nature had been drawn off, as happens in the case of a liquid, which, when the vessel enclosing it is broken, is scattered and disappears, since there is nothing which now contains it.

Now as the principle of death, becoming operative in

the case of one man, passed therewith throughout the whole of human nature, in like manner the principle of the resurrection through one man extends to all humanity.[1] For He Who again united to His own body the soul which He had assumed, by means of His own power which was commingled with each of them at their original constitution, on a more universal scale,[2] as it were, mingled the intelligent substance with the sensible, as the principle successfully makes its way in due sequence to the very end.

For when in the humanity [3] which He assumed the soul again returned to the body after the dissolution, the union of that which was severed, as it were by some new principle, extends potentially in an equal degree to the whole of human nature. And this is the mystery of GOD's design with regard to death and the resurrection from the dead; that while GOD has not prevented the soul from being separated from the body by death in the inevitable course of nature, yet He has brought them together again by the resurrection, in order that He Himself might become the meeting-point of both, that is of death and life, in His own person arresting [4] the process of dissolution effected in our nature by death, and Himself becoming a principle of reunion for the separated elements.

[1] Cp. Rom. v. 15 f.; 1 Cor. xv. 21.

[2] Or, as Mr. Colson has suggested, "rising from the individual to the *genus*." The words γενικωτέρῳ τινὶ λόγῳ are highly technical. The process of reuniting soul and body is extended from the individual case of Christ to the whole of humanity.

[3] ἀνθρώπῳ, here used loosely for "humanity."

[4] Mr. Colson suggests that a negative is required, "not arresting, . . . but Himself becoming." This would be parallel to the language of Gregory a few lines above.

CHAPTER XVII

[Gregory now deals with the objection already stated, " Why did not GOD restore man by a mere act of His will ? " A patient does not dictate the method of his cure. We must look to the beneficence of the result attained, and wait for fuller light.]

BUT it will be said that we have not yet removed the objection which has been submitted to us, and that the argument advanced against us by unbelievers is rather strengthened by what we have been saying. For if GOD possesses such power, as our argument has shown, that the destruction of death and the access to life both rest with Him, why does He not carry out His purpose by a simple act of will, instead of effecting our salvation by a round-about way, submitting to birth and nurture, and experiencing death while engaged in saving man, when He might have been exempt from these conditions and yet have saved us?

In reply to such an objection it might have been sufficient in dealing with reasonable persons to reply that the sick do not lay down to their physicians the method of their treatment, nor do they dispute with their benefactors about the manner in which they are to be cured, asking them why he who heals touched the ailing part, and why he devised this remedy to set them free from their trouble, whereas he ought to have employed a different remedy, but looking to the end which his good service has in view, they receive his kind attentions with thankfulness.

But since, as says the prophecy,[1] the abundance of GOD's kindness benefits us in a hidden manner, and is not clearly seen in the present life; for otherwise all the

---

[1] Ps. xxx. 19 (in the LXX. Ps. xxx. (xxxi.) 20, where the word ἔκρυψας is found).

E

objections of unbelievers would have been taken away, if that which we look for had been before our eyes ; whereas now it waits for the ages to come, so that in them there may be revealed the things which we now see by faith only ;—it will be necessary to employ certain arguments, as far as is possible, in order to find for the questions before us a solution in accordance with what has preceded.

CHAPTER XVIII

[Whatever be the manner of Christ's appearing, the testimony of history shows its effects.   The cessation of heathen worship, the spread of the Christian religion, the lives of the martyrs, the destruction of the Jewish temple and worship, all show Christ's Divine power.]

AND yet it is perhaps superfluous, if we have come to believe that GOD sojourned in human life, to criticize the manner of His presence, on the ground that it was not brought about in the way of what we think to be wisdom and superior reason. For those who are not bitterly hostile to the truth will find a proof of the Divine sojourn which is by no means inadequate, a proof which is manifested even before the future life in our present existence, I mean the testimony supplied by actual facts.

For who does not know how the deception practised by demons [1] had prevailed throughout every part of the world, gaining the mastery over the life of men through the madness of idolatry ; how this had become the custom among all nations throughout the world, to worship the demons under the form of idols by animal sacrifices and the pollutions offered upon their altars ?   But since,

---

[1] On the prevalent belief in demons see Glover, *Conflict of Religions in the Roman Empire* (for the teaching of Plutarch). The present passage recalls Athanasius, *de Inc.*, 13, 14.

as the Apostle says,[1] the grace of GOD, bringing salvation
to all men, has appeared, sojourning in our human nature,
they have all vanished like smoke into nothing, so that
the madness of their oracles and prophecies has ceased,
their annual processions and the bloody pollutions of their
hecatombs have been abolished, and amongst most
nations altars, porticoes, sacred precincts, shrines have
entirely disappeared,[2] together with all the other observances practised by the worshippers of the demons to the
deception both of themselves and of those whom they
came across, so that in many places there is no remem-
brance even that these things formerly existed; while in
their place there have arisen throughout the whole world,
in honour of the name of Christ, temples and altars and
the revered and unbloody priesthood,[3] and the sublime
philosophy,[4] the pursuit of which consists in action rather
than in words, and the disdain of the life of the body, and
the contempt for death [5] displayed by those whom tyrants
have sought to compel to abandon the faith, counting as
nothing the outrages inflicted upon the body and the
sentence of death, whereas they certainly would not have
endured these, had not the proof of the Divine sojourning
which they possessed been certain and beyond dispute.

Moreover the following fact is a sufficient indication,
in reply to the Jews, of the presence of Him in Whom they
disbelieve. For until the Divine appearing of Christ they
had before their eyes in all their splendour the palaces
in Jerusalem, that far-famed temple, their customary
yearly sacrifices; all that the Law had marked out in
veiled language for those who were able to understand

[1] Titus, ii. 11.

[2] Cp. a similar passage in Athanasius, *de Inc.*, 46 f.

[3] The term " unbloody sacrifice " (ἀναίμακτος θυσία) was
commonly applied to the Eucharist by Christian writers.

[4] The word φιλοσοφία was used by Christian writers sometimes of the monastic life, but also quite generally, as here,
to denote the practice of the Christian religion.

[5] Cp. Athanasius, *de Inc.*, 27.

their hidden meaning up till that time went on unhindered according to the ritual of their religion which had been enjoined upon them from the beginning. But when they saw Him Whom they looked for, of whom their prophets and the law had taught them beforehand, and when they chose, in preference to belief in Him Who had appeared, that which was henceforth a mistaken superstition, their false interpretation of which led them to keep the letter of the law, becoming the slaves of custom rather than intelligence, the result was that they refused to welcome the grace which had appeared, while the august rites of their worship survive in records only; their temple is no longer known even by any traces of it; their splendid city was left in ruins, so that there remains to the Jews none of their ancient observances enjoined by the law, while access to the holy spot in Jerusalem is denied to them by the decree of the rulers.[1]

CHAPTER XIX

[The reasonableness of the Incarnation is shown by its accordance with the attributes of GOD.]

HOWEVER, since neither those who follow Greek ways of thought nor the leaders of Jewish beliefs think fit to regard these things as proofs of a Divine presence, it will be well, in dealing with the objections brought against us, that our argument should clearly indicate why the Divine nature united itself with ours, saving humanity by its own presence, and not effecting its purpose by a command. What, then, shall we choose as a starting-point, that will conduct our argument by a proper chain of reasoning to the conclusion which we have in view? What other than a brief review of the conceptions of GOD which are in accord with piety?

[1] A reference to the decree of Hadrian, after the Jewish revolt, in 134 A.D., forbidding the Jews to dwell in Jerusalem.

CHAPTER XX

[*The perfection of the Divine Being involves His possession of power, justice, goodness, and wisdom. All these were exhibited in the Incarnation. How goodness and wisdom were shown in the recovery of man.*]

IT is generally agreed that we ought to believe that GOD not only possesses power, but also justice, goodness, wisdom, and everything else which suggests to the mind excellence. It follows then that, in that design of His which is before our notice, no one or other of the attributes of GOD should tend to be manifested in the history, while another is absent. For none of these lofty titles by itself alone and separated from the rest constitutes virtue as a whole. Good is not truly good, if it is not associated with what is just, wise, and powerful. For that which is unjust or unwise or wanting in power is not good. Nor is power regarded as a virtue, if it is separated from what is righteous and wise. For such a form of power is brutal and tyrannical. The same statement applies to the other attributes; if what is wise passes the bounds of what is just, or if what is just is unaccompanied by power and goodness, such instances would more properly be called vice. For how can that be numbered among good things which is lacking in excellence?

Now if in our ideas of GOD it is fitting that all these attributes should be combined, let us consider whether GOD's design with regard to man is lacking in the conceptions which befit His nature. What we are seeking in the case of GOD undoubtedly is signs of His goodness. And what clearer testimony can there be of goodness than the fact that He reclaimed him who had deserted to the enemy's side, and that the nature which is fixed in goodness and unchangeable was not affected by the changeable will of man? For He would not have come to save us, as David says,[1] were it not that His goodness suggested such a design.

But the goodness of this design would have been fruitless, if wisdom had not rendered His love towards man operative. For even in the case of those who are sick there are possibly many who wish that the sick man was not in so wretched a state, but only those bring their good purpose on behalf of the sick to a successful result, in whose case trained ability operates for the healing of the sick man. Wisdom, then, must undoubtedly be combined with goodness. How, then, do we see wisdom combined with goodness in the events which have come to pass? For it is not possible to discern goodness of purpose apart by itself. For how can the purpose be shown, unless it is manifested in facts? But the actual events, proceeding in due sequence in a certain orderly chain, show the wisdom and skill of GOD's design.

But since, as we have already said, it is wisdom only as combined with justice which constitutes virtue, whereas, if severed from it, it is not good in itself apart, it will be well also in discussing the design of GOD with regard to man to consider in conjunction with one another these two attributes, I mean wisdom and justice.

CHAPTER XXI

[*In this and the two following chapters Gregory shows how the justice of GOD was shown in the Incarnation. Man's mutable nature exposed him to change in the direction of good or evil, while his intelligence was liable to be misled in its discernment of good. How Satan deceived man and made him his prey.*]

How, then, is justice shown? We remember, doubtless, the points established in due sequence at the beginning

[1] Possibly a reference to such passages as Ps. cv. (cvi.) 4-5; cxviii. (cxix.) 65, 66, 68, in the Greek Bible.

of this treatise,[1] that man was created as a copy of the Divine nature and that he preserves his likeness to the Divine Being, not only in the other blessings which he enjoys, but also in his possession of free-will, though he has of necessity a nature subject to change. For it was not possible that he who owed the beginning of his existence to a change should be altogether free from the tendency to change. For the transition from nonentity to existence is a change, non-existence being changed by the Divine power into being. A further reason why change is necessarily seen in man, is that man was a copy of the Divine nature; and the copy, unless it presented some point of difference, would be altogether identical with that which it has been made to resemble.

The difference, then, between that which was made " in the image " and the original pattern lies in this, that the one is by nature incapable of change, while the other is not so, but as it was by a change that it came into existence (as we have shown above), so being subject to change it does not and cannot remain in its state of existence.

Now change is a kind of movement always proceeding from the state in which a thing is to a different state, and such a movement takes two forms. The one is always in the direction of good, and in this the advance cannot be arrested, because there is no limit to that which is explored. The other is in the contrary direction, and its essence consists in having no existence. For the contrast with the good, as we have said previously, implies something of the same idea of opposition as is implied when we say that that which exists is logically opposed to that which does not exist and existence to non-existence. Now in the tendency and movement towards variation and change it is not possible for the nature to remain independent and unmoved, but the will tends wholly in some one direction, because its

[1] See Chap. V.

desire for that which is good impels it naturally into movement.

Now the good is partly that which is truly and naturally such, and partly that which is decked out with a certain semblance of good. That which adjudicates between them is the mind, seated within us; and herein we run the risk either of gaining that which is really good, or of being diverted from it by some deceptive appearance and so being carried away to the opposite, just as the heathen fable says was the fate of the dog, who, turning away his eyes to the reflection in the water of that which he carried in his mouth, let go the real food, and, opening his mouth wide to swallow the image of it, was left in hunger.

The intelligence, then, being cheated of its desire for that which is really good, was led away to the non-existent, being persuaded by the guile of the instigator and discoverer of vice that that was good which was contrary to good (for the deception would have proved ineffectual, had not the semblance of good been spread upon the hook of vice like a bait); and man by his own decision involved himself in this misfortune, seeing that through pleasure he enslaved himself to the enemy of his life. Investigate now with me the attributes which are suitable to our conceptions of GOD, goodness, wisdom, justice, power, incorruption, and everything else which indicates excellence. As being good, then, He pities fallen man; as wise, He is not ignorant of the means for recalling him. It will be the part of wisdom further to discern what is just, for true justice can never be associated with folly.

CHAPTER XXII

|GOD'S justice was shown in His dealings with Satan. As man had voluntarily sold himself into slavery, justice required that he should be restored by the payment of a ransom which his owner was ready to accept.]

WHAT, then, in this case constitutes justice? The fact that He did not employ against him who held us in his power any tyrannical authority, or by superior power wrest us from him who held us, thus leaving him who had enslaved man through pleasure with a pretext for a just plea in his defence. For just as those who have sold their liberty for money are the slaves of their purchasers, seeing that they have constituted themselves the sellers of their own persons, and it is not permissible for them or any other person to claim liberty on their behalf, even though they who have reduced themselves to this unfortunate state are men of noble birth; while if some one through concern for him who has thus been sold were to use violence against the purchaser, he would be regarded as unjust in endeavouring to rescue by arbitrary means him who was legally acquired; whereas if he wished to buy back again such an one, there is no law to prevent him; in like manner, seeing that we had voluntarily sold ourselves, it was necessary that He Who in His goodness was seeking to rescue us and set us free should devise no arbitrary method of restoring us, but one that was consistent with justice. And some such method of this kind it is to put it within the power of him who was the master to receive whatever ransom he might wish as the price of him whom he held in his possession.

CHAPTER XXIII

[*How Satan was led to accept Christ as a ransom for mankind.*]

WHAT ransom, then, was it likely that the master would choose to receive? It is possible, following our train of thought, to form some conjecture of his desire, if the facts which are clear are used to point the way to that which we are seeking. He then who, according to the teaching propounded at the beginning of this treatise, had shut his eyes to the good through envy of man's happiness, and who had engendered in himself the gloom of vice, and who had contracted the ailment of the love of power, which is the origin and foundation of the inclination to evil and, as it were, the mother of all other forms of vice—what would he receive in exchange for him whom he held in possession, unless it were plainly something higher and better, in order to satisfy more completely his passion of pride by receiving more than he gave?

But among all the men of whom history tells from the beginning of the world he had never been conscious in any one of anything like that which he saw in Him Who appeared at that time, conception without sexual union, birth without corruption, a virgin giving suck to a child, and voices from the unseen world [1] testifying from above to surpassing worth, a mode of healing natural infirmities without trouble or the use of means, set in operation by a mere command and effort of will, the return of the dead to life, the deliverance of those possessed,[2] the fear inspired

[1] Luke ii. 10-14.

[2] τὴν τῶν καταδίκων ἀνάρρυσιν. The words are absent from many MSS. of Gregory. Literally they mean "the deliverance of those under condemnation." They have been variously interpreted: (1) the absolution of sinners; (2) the

in demons, His authority over the changes of the atmo-
sphere, His walking across the sea, the deep not parting
on either side and laying bare its foundation for those
who passed through, as in the miracle of Moses, but the
surface of the water above presenting a solid ground to His
tread, and by a kind of firm resistance supporting His
steps; His disregard for food as long as He willed, and
the bounteous feasts in the wilderness by which many
thousands were well fed, though neither the heaven poured
down manna upon them, nor did the earth supply their
needs by providing food from her own natural products,
but this liberality proceeded from the ineffable store-
houses of the Divine power, the bread being produced
ready in the hands of those who distributed it, and
multiplying the more, as those who ate of it were filled;
the feeding of them with fishes, though the sea did not
contribute to their need, but He Who spread the tribe
of fishes through the sea.

And how can each of the Gospel miracles be passed in
review? Seeing, then, this power, the enemy saw that
in Him more was proposed in the bargain than he held.
Therefore he chose Him as the ransom price for those
who were shut up in the prison house of death.[1] But
it would have been impossible for him to look upon the
unveiled appearance of GOD, had he not seen in Him
some portion of that flesh which already he had taken
captive through sin. On this account the Deity was
clothed with the flesh, in order that by looking at what was
familiar and akin to him, he might not be affrighted at the
near approach of the superior power, and perceiving the
power which shone out quietly more and more through

deliverance of those who were subject to deadly diseases;
(3) the casting out of devils. In the text (3) has been
adopted. The words cannot refer, as Krabinger suggests,
to the final restitution of all sinners.

[1] For this idea, which is found in Origen and later Fathers,
see Introduction, p. 16 f.

the miracles, he might think that that which appeared to him was an object of desire rather than of fear.[1]

You see how goodness is combined with justice, and wisdom is not separated from them. For by the device which enabled the Divine power to become capable of apprehension by being clothed with the body, in order that His design with regard to us might not be hindered through fear of the Divine manifestation, there is demonstrated the union of all these attributes, goodness, wisdom, justice. For that He chose to save us is a testimony of His goodness; that He made the redemption of him who was held in bondage a matter of exchange shows His justice; that He made the enemy by His device capable of apprehending that which is beyond all apprehension is a proof of the highest wisdom.

CHAPTER XXIV

[*The Divine power was shown more clearly by GOD'S condescension in the Incarnation than by all the wonders of Creation. Its result was to bring light and life to man.*]

BUT it is natural that he who carefully attends to the course of our previous argument should inquire where the power of the Godhead, where the incorruptibility of the Divine power, is seen in the facts which we have narrated. In order, then, that this too may be made clear, let us consider the sequel of the Gospel revelation, in which power in conjunction with love to man is most clearly seen.[2]

---

[1] The idea that the humanity of Christ served as a screen to hide His Godhead from Satan occurs in Gregory of Nazianzus, and is hinted at still earlier by Ignatius, *Eph.* xix. It may be based upon 1 Cor. ii. 8.

[2] For the idea compare the language of the Gelasian Collect (H. A. Wilson, *Gelasian Sacramentary*, p. 227), " Deus

In the first place, then, the fact that the omnipotent nature should have been capable of descending to the low estate of humanity provides a clearer proof of power than great and supernatural miracles. For that the Divine power should effect something great and transcendent is in a way in accordance with its nature and consistent with it. And we should not be uttering anything startling to the ears, if we were to say that the whole creation comprised in the universe, and all that is apprehended outside the visible world, derived its constitution from the power of GOD, the very will of GOD assuming substantial existence according to His pleasure. But the descent to our low estate is a surpassing display of His power which is in no way impeded even in conditions opposed to nature.

It is the peculiar character of the essence of fire to mount upwards, and that which is a natural operation in the case of a flame would not excite wonder; whereas if the flame were seen streaming downwards, like heavy bodies, such an occurrence would be regarded as marvellous, how, that is, fire, while remaining fire, surpasses its nature in the manner of its movement, by its downward tendency. So also in the case of the Divine and transcendent power neither the great expanses of the heavens, nor the bright beams of its luminaries, nor the ordering of the universe and the unceasing direction of existing things, exhibit this power so clearly as the condescension to the weakness of our nature, how, that is, the lofty, coming to exist in lowliness, is seen in this lowliness, and yet descends not from its height, how Deity enfolding itself in human nature both becomes this, and is that.

For since, as we have already said, it was not in the

---

qui omnipotentiam tuam parcendo maxime et miserando manifestas," reproduced in the English Prayer Book Collect for the Eleventh Sunday after Trinity.

nature of the hostile power to come into contact with the untempered presence of GOD and endure His unveiled appearance, in order that He might be within the easy grasp of him who sought the exchange on our behalf, the Divine Being concealed Himself with the veil of our nature, that, just as is the case with greedy fish, the hook of the Deity might be swallowed along with the bait of the flesh,[1] and so, when life had been domiciled with death, and light had shone upon darkness, that which is the opposite of light and life might vanish away. For it is not in the nature of darkness to remain when light is present, nor of death to exist where life is in activity.

Let us then resume, by way of brief summary, the course of the argument for the Christian revelation, and so complete our defence of it against those who accuse GOD's design because the Deity effects the salvation of mankind by a personal intervention. For the Divine Being must exhibit throughout the attributes which are befitting to Him, and we may not form a lofty conception of one attribute, while another attribute of the proper dignity of GOD is excluded; but every lofty and devout thought must without reserve be included in our belief with regard to GOD, and the one must be connected with the other in due sequence.

We have shown, then, that goodness, wisdom, justice, power, incapacity for corruption, are all exhibited in the doctrine of GOD's design with regard to us. Goodness is apprehended in His choosing to save him who was lost. Wisdom and justice were shown in His manner of saving us; power in the fact that He came in the likeness and fashion of man in the lowly condition of our nature, and in the hope inspired that, like other men, He could be held fast in the power of death; it was shown again in the fact that, though He had become such, He effected that which properly belongs to Himself and is in accord-

[1] Similar language is used by Rufinus, *Comm. in Symb. Ap.* 16, and Gregory the Great (*Mor.* xxxiii. 7).

ance with His nature. Now the proper characteristic of
light is to banish darkness, and of life to destroy death.
Since, then, in wandering astray from the right path at
the beginning we had turned away from life and become
involved in death, what is there improbable in the teaching
which we receive from the Gospel revelation, if purity
lays hold of those who were defiled by sin, and life lays
hold of the dead, and guidance is given to those who
have gone astray, in order that the defilement may be
cleansed, and the error set right, and the dead return to
life?

CHAPTER XXV

*[The Incarnation justified by the analogy of GOD'S immanence
in Creation.]*

Now that the Deity should come to be in our nature
will not on any reasonable grounds seem a strange idea
to those who do not take a very narrow view of existence.
For who is so simple-minded as not to believe, when he
considers the universe, that the Divine Being is in everything, clothing Himself with it, embracing it, and residing
in it? For all things depend upon Him Who is, and it
is not possible for anything to exist which does not have
its being in Him Who is. If, then, all things are in Him,
and He in all things, why are they ashamed of the plan
of our religion which teaches that GOD came to be in
man, seeing that we believe that not even now is He
outside man? [1]

For if the manner in which GOD is present in us is not
the same as it was in that case, yet it is none the less
admitted that now, as then, He is equally in us. Now
He is commingled with us, in that He maintains nature
in existence. Then He mingled Himself with our nature,

---

[1] The appeal to the immanence of GOD in creation is also
found in Athanasius, *de Inc.*, 41–42. See Introduction. pp.
15, 18.

in order that by this mingling with the Divine Being our nature might become divine, being delivered from death and set free from the tyranny of the adversary. For His return from death becomes to this race of mortals the beginning of the return to the immortal life.

CHAPTER XXVI

[The deception of Satan by the veiling of the Deity in Christ was an act of just retribution. But it also served a purpose of love. Satan will be purged by the refining fire of the Divine Power and led to acknowledge the justice and saving work of GOD.]

BUT perhaps, in examining the justice and wisdom which are observed in this Divine plan, some one may be led to think that such a method devised on our behalf by GOD is a form of deceit. For that GOD put Himself in the power of him who had the mastery over us, not in His unveiled Deity, but clothed with the covering of human nature, and so passed unrecognized by the adversary, is, in a way, a kind of deceit and trickery, since it is a characteristic of those who deceive that they divert the expectations of those against whom they conspire to one thing, and then bring about another, different from what they expected. But he who looks to the truth will recognize that here, too, there is a supreme display of Divine justice and wisdom.

For it is the mark of justice to render to every one according to his desert, and of wisdom neither to pervert justice, nor to separate from the decisions of justice the gracious purpose of love to man, but skilfully to combine them both; in justice, making a proper recompense, in goodness, not departing from the purpose of love to man. Let us consider, then, whether these two attributes are not observed in the events described.

For the action of rewarding the deceiver according to his desert, by deceiving him in turn, is a display of justice, while the purpose with which it was done is a testimony to the goodness of Him Who effected it. For it is the characteristic of justice to render to each man those results whose origins and causes he has previously planted,[1] just as the earth yields her fruits according to the character of the seeds sown in it; while it is characteristic of wisdom, in the way in which it renders like for like, not to lose sight of the higher aim. The conspirator and he who sets himself to heal the victim of the conspiracy both alike mix a drug with the man's food, but in the one case it is a poison, in the other an antidote to the poison; the manner of the cure in no way impairs the aim of the kindly act. For even though in both cases there is a mixture of a drug in food, yet considering the purpose in view, we bestow praise in the one case, and feel indignation in the other. So also in the present case, on the principle of justice, the deceiver receives in turn that very treatment the seeds of which he had sown by his own free-will. For he who had previously deceived man with the bait of pleasure is himself deceived by the screen of humanity. But the purpose of the action changes its character and makes it good.

For the one exercised his deceit in order to ruin our nature, but He Who is at once just and good and wise employed His deceitful device for the salvation of him who had been ruined, benefiting by these means not only him who was lost, but also the very author of our ruin.[2] For from the contact of death with life, of darkness with light, of corruption with incorruption, there resulted a disappearance of the worse element and its passage into a state of non-existence, and the benefiting of him who is purged from these ills.

[1] Gregory has in mind Gal. vi. 7.
[2] The source of this conception is Origen (de Princ., iii. 6; cp. i. 6). See Introduction, p. 16.

F

˙When a baser material is mixed with gold, the refiners [1] of the gold make the foreign and worthless element to disappear by consuming it with fire, and so restore the more precious material to its natural brightness. The severance, indeed, is not brought about without difficulty, seeing that time is needed for the fire, with its destructive power, to cause the spurious metal to disappear; yet this melting away of that element, whose presence in it impairs the beauty of the gold, is a kind of cure applied to the latter. In like manner, when death, corruption, darkness, and all the other products of vice had attached themselves to the nature of the author of evil, the approach of the Divine power, acting like fire, effects the disappearance of the element which was contrary to nature, and, by thus purging it, benefits the nature, even though the sifting process proves painful. Hence even the adversary himself would not dispute the justice and salutary effect of that which was done, if he possibly might perceive the benefit bestowed on him.

For in the present life those who are subjected to the knife or caustics in order to cure them, grow angry with their physicians, smarting under the pain of the incision; whereas if by these means they regain health, and the pain of the cautery passes away, they will be grateful to those who effected the cure in them.[2] In like manner, when by these long and circuitous methods the evil, which is now mingled with our nature and has become a part of its growth, has been finally expelled from it, and when those who are now plunged in vice are restored to their original state,[3] a chorus of thanksgiving will arise from all creation, not only from the lips of those

[1] For this teaching on the purification of souls, see Introduction, p. 13 f. The " refiner's fire " is found in Origen, c. Cels., vi. 44.

[2] Origen (c. Cels., vi. 56) uses the same illustration of the remedial chastisements of God.

[3] On the restoration of all souls, another Origenistic feature in the present work, see Introduction, p. 13 f.

who have endured the chastening of this purification, but also from those who never needed such purification at all.

This and the like teaching is contained in the great mystery of the Divine Incarnation. For by mingling with humanity, and sharing all the characteristics of our nature, birth, nurture, growth, going even so far as to experience death, He effected all the results that we have previously described, delivering man from vice and healing the very author of vice.[1] For the healing of an ailment consists in the purging of the disease, even though the process is painful.

CHAPTER XXVII

[*The cleansing of our nature involved its complete assumption. A " heavenly body " would not have sufficed. Man needed to be touched in order to be healed. All created things whether in heaven or on earth are equally below the Divine transcendence. The one thing that is consistent with GOD'S character is to succour the needy.*]

IT is quite consistent that He Who infused Himself into our nature should accept this union with us in all the properties of that nature. For they who wash off the filth of garments do not leave some of the stains, while washing away others, but cleanse the whole texture of the garment from its stains from beginning to end, in order that the garment may become entirely uniform in character, glistening throughout as a result of its washing. So, when human life had been defiled by sin in its beginning and end and all that lies between, the power which cleansed it must traverse the whole extent, and not apply its purifying treatment to one part, while leaving

[1] How the benefits of the Incarnation are applied to Satan Gregory does not discuss.

the other without treatment. Since, then, our life is embraced within two limits, one on either side, I mean the beginning and the end, the power which amends our nature is found at either extremity, laying hold of the beginning, extending to the end, and embracing all that lies between.

Now since there is one manner of entering into life for all men, how was it necessary for Him Who was entering in unto us to become domiciled in this life? "From heaven"[1] is perhaps the reply of him who regards with loathing the form of human birth as being shameful and inglorious. But in heaven there was no human nature, and in the super-terrestrial life the disease of vice did not prevail. But He Who mingled Himself with man effected this union with the aim of benefiting us. How, then, does any one seek in that abode, where evil was not, and where human life was not lived, the humanity with which GOD was clothed, or rather not humanity, but some image and semblance of man? What amendment of our nature could have resulted, if, when it was this earthly creature who was ailing, some heavenly being had received the commingling of the Divine. For he who is sick cannot be cured unless the ailing part specially receives the healing.

If, then, the sick part was on earth, and if the Divine power had not been applied to that sick part out of respect for its own proper dignity, the occupation of the Divine power with objects which have nothing in common with us would not have profited man. For the indignity in the case of the Deity would have been equally great, if it is legitimate to conceive of anything except vice as an indignity to GOD. But he who in a narrow spirit judges that the Divine majesty consists in the fact that

---

[1] The belief here referred to was current in the time of Gregory, and was attributed, though without justification, to Apollinaris. See Vincent of Lerins, *Common.*, xii. (17); Tixeront, *Histoire des Dogmes*, II. 100 f.

it does not admit of participation in the properties of our nature, does not find the dishonour lessened by the fact that the Deity took the form of a heavenly body rather than an earthly one. For all creation is equally remote from and below the Most High, Who is inaccessible by reason of the transcendence of His nature, and the whole universe is in the same rank of inferiority below Him. For He Who is wholly inaccessible, is not accessible to one part, and unapproachable by another, but equally transcends all existing things.

Earth, then, is not further removed from His dignity, nor heaven closer to it, and the beings who inhabit each of these elements do not differ from one another in this respect, so that the one are in contact with the inaccessible nature, while the others are separated from it; otherwise we should suspect that the Power which governs the universe did not equally pervade all things, but super-abounds in some portions and is lacking in others, and on account of this difference of measure and degree the Divine Being will in consequence appear to be composite and incongruous, if we suppose it to be remote from us, so far as its nature is concerned, but adjacent to some other creature, and in consequence of its nearness easily apprehended.

But the true view in regard to that transcendent dignity looks neither below nor above by way of comparison; for all things are equally beneath the Power which presides over the universe, so that if the earthly nature is thought to be unworthy of union with the Divine Being, no other can be found to possess such worth. But if all things equally fall short of that dignity, one thing alone accords with GOD's character, that is, to succour the needy. If then we confess that, where there was disease, there the healing power resorted, in what way does our belief lie outside the conception which we ought to form of GOD?

CHAPTER XXVIII

*[Gregory vindicates the constitution of the human body, and
urges that there was no dishonour to GOD involved in
His entering upon human life by the process of birth.]*

BUT they ridicule our nature and harp upon the manner
of our birth, and think in this way to hold up our religion
to scorn, as though it were unbecoming for GOD to come
into contact and fellowship with human life by such an
entrance. But we have already dealt with this in previous
discussions, showing that the only thing which is disgraceful in itself is evil and whatsoever is akin to vice.
But the course of nature, being ordered by the will and
law of GOD, is far removed from the accusation of vice,
otherwise the charge brought against nature would recoil
upon the Creator, if anything connected with it were
accused of being shameful and unbecoming.

If, then, the Divine Being is separate from vice alone,
and nature is not identical with vice, and our religion
asserts that GOD was born in man, and not in vice, and
if there is but one way for man to enter upon life, that
through which the child which is generated passes into
existence, what other method of passing into life do they
lay down for GOD, seeing that they admit that it is reasonable that the nature which has been weakened by vice
should be visited by the Divine power, though they are
offended at the manner of His visitation, not knowing
that the whole structure of the human body is of equal
value in all its parts, and that nothing in it which con-
tributes to the maintenance of life can be accused of being
dishonourable or evil?

For the whole equipment of the organism of the body
has been designed with one end in view, and that end is
to preserve humanity in existence. Now the other organs

maintain the present life of man, sharing among themselves different activities, by means of which the faculty
of perception and action is exercised, but the generative
organs have in view provision for the future, introducing
in turn, by their mediation, a continuous succession to
our nature.

If, then, you look at the matter with a view to utility,
to which of the organs commonly recognized as honourable will they yield first place?[1] Which of them would
they not, with good reason, be judged to surpass in
honour? For it is not by the eye, or the ear, or any
other of the organs of sense that our race is continually
maintained. For these faculties, as we have said, have
to do with present enjoyment, but in those organs immortality is preserved for humanity, so that death, which
is ever actively at work against us, is, in a way, rendered
ineffectual and fruitless, since by means of the succeeding
generations nature is constantly introducing itself in turn
to fill up the gap. What is there, then, unworthy of GOD
in the contents of our religion, if GOD mingled Himself
with human life by those means which nature employs
to fight against death?

CHAPTER XXIX

*[Gregory discusses the question why the Incarnation was so
long delayed.]*

BUT leaving this objection, our opponents attempt by
other means also to find fault with our teaching, and ask
why, if what took place was good and worthy of GOD,
did He postpone the benefit?[2] Why did He not cut

---

[1] An echo of 1 Cor. xii. 23 f.
[2] Athanasius deals with the same question in *Or. c. Ar.*,
i. 29; ii. 68.

short the further progress of vice, while it was yet in its beginnings?

To this we make the brief reply that the postponement of the benefit was due to wisdom and foresight of what was profitable to our nature. For even in bodily diseases, when some corrupt humour steals beneath the pores, before the unnatural secretion has entirely come to light upon the surface, those who apply trained methods to ailments do not treat it with drugs which close up the body, but wait for that which lurks within to come out in its whole extent, and then when the malady is fully revealed they apply their cure. When, then, the disease of vice had seized upon the nature of humanity, the Physician of the universe waited until no form of wickedness was left concealed in our nature.

Therefore He did not apply His cure to man immediately after Cain's envy and murder of his brother. For the wickedness of those who were destroyed in the time of Noah had not yet broken forth, nor had the grievous disease of Sodom's lawlessness been revealed, nor the war of the Egyptians against GOD, nor the pride of the Assyrians, nor the blood-guiltiness of the Jews against the saints of GOD, nor Herod's lawless slaughter of the children, nor all the other deeds which are either recorded, or, though not recorded, were done in the succeeding ages, seeing that the root of evil puts forth many different kinds of shoots in the wills of man. When, then, vice had reached its furthest limit, and no kind of evil was any longer left which man had not attempted, in order that the treatment might reach through the whole extent of the ailment, it was not at its beginning, but when it had come to full development, that GOD cured the disease.

CHAPTER XXX

*[Gregory answers two further objections. (1) " Why has
  not sin ceased since the Incarnation ? " (2) " Why
  has not grace come to all men ? "]*

BUT if any one thinks to refute our teaching by the
objection that even after the treatment has been applied
human life is still impaired by sins, let him be guided to
the truth by a well-known illustration.   When a serpent
has received its death-blow on the head, the coil is not
immediately killed with the head, but though the latter
is dead, the tail part is still animated by the principle of
life peculiar to it and is not deprived of its vital motion.
So also we may see sin dealt a mortal blow, but still in
its remnants harassing the life of man.

But though they cease to find fault with the teaching
of our religion in this respect also, they make it a charge
against our faith that it does not reach all men.   " Why
is it," they ask, " that the grace of the Gospel has not
come to all men, but while some have attached themselves to the teaching, no small portion of humanity
remains unaffected, either because GOD did not will to
bestow the benefit on all ungrudgingly, or because He
was quite incapable of doing so ? "   Neither of these
suppositions is free from blame.   For it is not consistent
with GOD's character that He should not will what is
good or that He should be incapable of performing
it.   " If, then, the Faith is a good thing, why," they
urge, " has not the grace of the Gospel come to all
men ? "

Now if in the course of our argument we had taken
up the position that the Divine will deals out faith at
random to men, some being called, and the rest having
no part in the call, there would have been occasion for

bringing such a charge against our religion. But if the call was addressed equally to all, without distinction of rank or age or difference of nationality—for on this account at the very first preaching of the Gospel[1] the ministers of the word were able all at once, by Divine inspiration, to speak in the languages of all nations, so that no one might be excluded from the blessings of their teaching—how, then, can any one with any show of reason make it a reproach against GOD that the teaching has not won its way among all men?

For He Who wields authority over the universe, by reason of the exceeding honour in which He held man, has left something in our own power, of which each of us is master. And this is the will, a faculty free from bondage and possessing the power of choice, seated in the independence of the mind. Such an accusation, then, might with greater justice be turned back upon those who have not attached themselves to the faith rather than upon Him Who invited them to assent to it. For neither when Peter[2] at the beginning preached the word in a numerous gathering of Jews, though three thousand at once welcomed the faith, did those who disbelieved, though more numerous than those who had believed, find fault with the Apostle because they had not been convinced. For it would not have been reasonable, when the grace of the Gospel had been set forth before all, that he who of his own accord held aloof should accuse another for his failure to share in it, rather than himself.

[1] Acts ii. 8–11. [2] Acts ii. 41.

CHAPTER XXXI

*[A further reply to the second of the two objections stated in
the previous chapter. Had God compelled belief, He
would have destroyed free-will. It is the disposition of
the hearers which is responsible for the fact that all
have not become believers.]*

BUT they have no difficulty in finding a captious reply
even to such arguments as these. For they say that
GOD might, if he wished, have applied compulsion to
lead those who resisted to receive the preaching. Where,
then, would free-will be in that case? And where virtue?
Where the praise due to those who succeed? For it is
only inanimate or irrational creatures whose characteristic
it is to be led by the will of another to do what he wants.
But the rational and intelligent nature, if it lay aside
its free-will, loses at the same time its privilege of belong-
ing to the intellectual order. For what use will he make
of his faculty of mind, if his power of choosing anything
according to his inclination is placed at the disposal of
another?

Moreover, if the will remains inactive, virtue of necessity there and then disappears, seeing that it is prevented
by the inactivity of the will. And when virtue ceases to
exist, life straightway loses its honour, the praise of
virtuous actions is taken away, sin may be indulged with
impunity, and all difference as to the mode of living becomes indiscernible. For who could reasonably any longer
find fault with the profligate, or praise him who shows self-
control, seeing that this answer would come readily to
every one, that nothing which we purpose to do is in our
power, but the wills of men are directed by a superior
power according to the pleasure of one who is their
master. Hence it is not the goodness of GOD which must

be charged with the fact that faith has not become planted in all men, but rather the disposition of those who receive the preaching.

CHAPTER XXXII

[The death of Christ necessary.   The mystic teaching of the Cross, and the Divine power shown in the Resurrection.]

WHAT further objection, in addition to the foregoing, do our adversaries still urge? That the transcendent nature, by preference, ought not to have undergone the experience of death [1] in any case, but even apart from this, by the superabundance of His power He might easily have effected His purpose. But if it was really necessary for this to happen for some inscrutable reason, yet at any rate He ought not to have been subject to the indignity of a shameful method of death. For, it is urged, what death could be more shameful than that through the Cross?

What, then, do we say to this? That the birth renders the death necessary. For He Who had once decided to share our humanity must inevitably pass through all the conditions proper to that nature. If, then, since human life is embraced within two limits, He had passed through the one and not come in contact with the other, His purpose would have remained but half complete, since He would not have come in touch with one of the states characteristic of our nature.

But possibly some one, with an exact knowledge of our religion, might urge with greater reason that the death did not happen because of the birth, but that on the contrary the birth was accepted for the sake of the

[1] Athanasius deals with the reasons for the death of Christ in *de Inc.*, 21–25.

death. For it was not because He Who ever is [1] needed to enter into life that He submitted to a birth in the body, but because He was recalling us from death to life. Since, then, it was necessary that the return of the whole of our nature from death should be brought about, stretching out a hand, as it were, to him who lay prone, He stooped to our dead body and approached death in such a way that He might come in contact with mortality, and in His own body provide our nature with a starting-point for the resurrection, raising up along with Him the whole man.

For since the Man [2] Who was the receptacle of the Godhead derived His being from no other source than the lump [3] of our humanity, even He Who through the resurrection was exalted along with His Godhead, just as in the case of our bodies the action of one of the organs of sense communicates a common sensation to the whole organism which is united with the particular part, so, inasmuch as the whole of our human nature forms, as it were, a single living being,[4] the resurrection of the part extends to the whole, and in virtue of the continuity and unity of the nature communicates itself from the part to the whole. What, then, is there outside the range of probability in the teaching of our religion, if He Who stands upright stoops to him who had fallen, in order to raise him up from his fall? But if the Cross contains any other deeper teaching, perhaps it is known to those

---

[1] For this phrase cp. Ex. iii. 14; Rev. i. 8.

[2] This language is inexact according to later theological standards. But Gregory is writing before Nestorianism had arisen.

[3] φυράματος. Cp. Rom. ix. 21; xi. 16; 1 Cor. v. 7.

[4] καθάπερ ἑνός τινος ὄντος ζῴου πάσης τῆς φύσεως. The idea is suggested by Plato's view of the universe as a "living being" (*Timaeus*, 30, 69C.). Neoplatonism carried on this teaching. Similarly the Stoics held that there was a συμπάθεια, or "sympathetic affection" between the different parts of nature and the universe.

who are skilled in mystical teaching. In any case, the teaching which has come down to us from tradition is to the following effect.

In the Gospel all words and actions have a higher and more divine meaning, and there is nothing which does not possess this character, and which does not reveal itself absolutely as a kind of mixture of the Divine with the human element. The utterance or the action proceeds in human fashion, while the mystical sense reveals the Divine element. It follows, then, that in this part of the Gospel too, while having regard to the one element, we should not pass over the other, but while seeing the human element in the death, in the manner of the death we should carefully seek the Divine. Now it is the characteristic of the Deity to pervade all things and to extend throughout the nature of existing things in every part. For nothing can remain in being, without remaining in Him Who exists, and that which in the proper and primary sense exists is the Divine nature, which the permanence of existing things of necessity compels us to believe to be in all things. We are taught by the Cross,[1] the figure of which is divided into four parts, so that from the centre, where the whole converges, the projections are four in number, that He Who was stretched thereon, at the time when the Divine plan was accomplished by His death, is He Who binds and unites the universe to Himself, bringing in His own Person the different kinds of existing things to one accord and harmony. For in existing things we have the conception of something above or below, or thought passes to the boundaries on either side. If, then, you consider the constitution of things in heaven, or below the earth, or those which are at either extremity of the universe,

---

[1] There is a similar exposition of the significance of the Cross in Athanasius, *de Inc.*, 25, and in Lactantius, *Div. Inst.*, iv. 26. It is a favourite conceit of the Fathers to trace the symbolism of the Cross in nature.

everywhere your thought is met in advance by the Deity,[1] Who alone is observed in existing things in every part, and Who maintains all things in being.

Whether this nature ought to be called Deity, or Reason, or Power, or Wisdom, or by any other of the exalted titles which are capable of expressing transcendence, our argument does not dispute about an expression, or title, or form of phrase. Since, then, the whole creation looks to Him and finds in Him its centre, and through Him acquires cohesion, the parts above being through Him connected with the parts below, and the opposite sides with one another, it was necessary that not by the ear alone should we be guided to the knowledge of GOD, but that sight also should be the teacher of sublime thoughts. From this also it is that the great Paul starts when he initiates [2] the people of Ephesus, and implants in them by his teaching the power to know what is "the depth and the height, and the breadth and the length." For he mentions each projection of the Cross by its own proper title, speaking of the upper part as "height," and the lower part as "depth," and the extensions on either side as "breadth" and "length." [3] And elsewhere, in addressing the Philippians,[4] he brings out, I think, some such thought still more clearly, when he says to them that "at the name of Jesus Christ every knee shall bow, of things in heaven and things on earth and things under the earth." There he embraces in one term the central cross-beam, and speaks of all that lies between the things in heaven and the things under the earth as that which is "on earth."

[1] For the idea cp. Ps. cxxxix. 6–10.

[2] μυσταγωγεῖ. A figure derived from the heathen mysteries. Ignatius (*Eph.* 12) similarly speaks of the Ephesians as "initiated along with Paul." The word μυεῖν is used by St. Paul in Phil. iv. 12.

[3] This interpretation of Eph. iii. 18 is found in Irenæus, Rufinus, Augustine and other Fathers.

[4] Phil. ii. 10.

Such is the mystery which we have been taught with
regard to the Cross. The events which follow in the
account are so consistent in character, that even unbelievers admit that there is nothing in them which is
foreign to the conception which we ought to form of
God. That He did not abide in death, and that the
wounds inflicted on His body by the spear [1] proved no
obstacle to His existence,[2] and that after His resurrection He appeared at His will to the disciples, and
whenever He chose was present among them without
being seen,[3] and came into their midst, needing no means
of entrance through the doors,[4] and that He strengthened
the disciples by breathing upon them the Spirit,[5] and
that He promised to be with them,[6] and that there
should be nothing to separate Him from them, and how
to the outward eye He ascended to heaven, while to the
mind He was everywhere present, and all the other
similar facts contained in the history, these need no
help from arguments to show that they are Divine and
belong to the sublime and transcendent Power. There
is no need, I imagine, for me to deal with them in detail,
for the narrative itself indicates that they are above
nature. But since a part of the doctrines of revelation
is concerned with the Divine plan with regard to the
washing (whether we wish to call it baptism, or illumina-
tion, or regeneration, we do not dispute as to the name),
it will be well briefly to discuss this also.

---

[1] John xix. 34.

[2] πρὸς τὸ εἶναι. A reference to the resurrection state.
Some MSS. read ἀναστῆναι.

[3] Luke xxiv. 36.   [4] John xx. 19.

[5] John xx. 22.   [6] Matt. xxviii. 20.

CHAPTER XXXIII

[Of the new birth of Baptism and the means by which it is effected. It is as mysterious as natural birth, and depends upon the working of the Divine power using natural means for a higher end.]

OUR opponents hear from us some statement of this kind, that when the mortal being passed into life, it was consistent that, since the first birth leads to a mortal existence, another birth should be devised which neither has its beginning in corruption nor ends in corruption, but conducts him who is born to immortal life, in order that, just as in consequence of a mortal birth that which was born was constituted mortal, so in consequence of the birth which does not admit of corruption that which is born may rise superior to the corruption resulting from death. When, then, they hear these and the like statements, and when they have previously been instructed as to the manner, that prayer to GOD, invocation of the heavenly grace, water, and faith, are the means by which the mystery [1] of regeneration is accomplished, they are incredulous, looking only at what the eye sees, on the ground that the material act does not coincide with the Divine promise. For, say they, how do prayer and the invocation of the Divine power, when made over the water, become to the initiated a source of life?

In reply to them, unless their opposition is of a very persistent kind, a simple argument suffices to bring them into agreement with our doctrine. For let us ask them in our turn, since the manner of carnal generation is

---

[1] μυστήριον. On the use of this term in connexion with the Sacraments, see Inge, *Christian Mysticism*, p. 253.

G

clear to all, how that which is implanted as the beginning of the constitution of a living being becomes a man. Yet surely in that case there is no theory which by any process of reasoning discovers the probable explanation. For what is there in common, when we compare the one with the other, between the definition of a man and the quality which we observe in that seed? Man is a being endowed with reason and intelligence, capable of thought and knowledge, whereas that seed is seen to possess a certain quality of moistness, and the mind grasps nothing further than what the senses perceive.

The reply, then, which it is probable may be given by those whom we asked how it is credible that a man should be constituted out of that element, is also the reply which we shall give when asked about the regeneration that is effected through the water. For in the former case each of those whom we ask may readily answer that it is by the Divine power that that element becomes a man, seeing that, if the Divine power is not present, it remains inert and ineffective. If, then, in the former case it is not the matter [1] which produces the man, but the Divine power which changes the visible material into the nature of a man, it would be the height of unreason that those who acknowledge such great power in God in that case should think that the Divine Being is powerless in this respect to carry out His will.

"What," they say, "is there in common between water and life?" "What is there in common," we shall reply to them, "between this quality of moistness and the image of God?" But in that case there is nothing extraordinary, if, when God so wills, that moist element changes into the most precious of living beings. In like manner in this case also we maintain that there is nothing wonderful if the presence of the Divine power transforms

---

[1] τὸ ὑποκείμενον, in its Aristotelian sense of "matter" as opposed to "form."

into a state of incorruption that which was born in a
nature subject to corruption.

CHAPTER XXXIV

*[The presence of the Divine Being, when invoked in Bap-
tism, is due to Christ's promise to be present in this
way. That He Who made the promise is Divine is
shown by miracles.]*

BUT they ask for proof of the presence of the Divine
Being when invoked to consecrate the rite. Let him
who seeks for this read again our previous investiga-
tions. For the proof which we gave that the power
which was manifested to us through the flesh was truly
Divine supports our present argument.

When we showed that He Who was manifested in the
flesh was GOD, since He revealed His own nature in the
miracles exhibited in the events of His life, we showed
at the same time that He is present at what is done
every time that He is invoked. For just as every existing thing has some characteristic of its own which indicates its nature, so the characteristic of the Divine
nature is truth. Now He has promised that He will be
present with those who call upon Him,[1] that He is in
the midst of those who believe,[2] and abides among them
all,[3] and has intercourse with each.[4] Hence we shall
need no further proof of the presence of the Divine
Being in the rite of Baptism, if the miracles have already
led us to believe that He is GOD; if, further, we know
that it is a characteristic of the Deity to be free from
all falsehood; and if we do not doubt that the thing

---

[1] Matt. vii. 7; John xiv. 13, etc.
[2] Matt. xviii. 20; xxviii. 20.
[3] John xv. 4 f.   [4] John xiv. 23.

which He has promised is there in virtue of the unfailing truth of the promise.

The fact that the invocation by prayer precedes the Divine design constitutes a superabundant proof that the act which is done is effected by GOD. For if in the other form of procreation of man the impulses of the parents, even though the Divine Being is not invoked by them in prayer, with the help of the Divine power, as we have previously said, fashion the child who is engendered—for without that power their effort is inoperative and useless—how much more in the spiritual mode of generation will the result aimed at be fully attained, seeing that GOD has promised to be present at what is done, and has put, as we believe, the power which proceeds from Himself in the act; since, further, our will is directed towards the object at which we aim, and if at the same time the help that comes through prayer is duly invited?

Those who pray to GOD that the sun may shine upon them, do not impair the effect of that which happens in any case, yet no one will say that the zeal of those who pray is useless, if they intreat GOD for that which will happen in any case. So those who are persuaded that, according to the unfailing truth of His promise, grace is present to those who are regenerated through this sacramental dispensation,[1] either make some addition to the grace, or do not divert that which exists. For we believe that the grace is present with them in any case because He Who gave the promise is GOD, while the testimony to His Deity is given through the miracles. Thus the presence of the Divine Being throughout admits of no dispute.

[1] τῆς μυστικῆς ταύτης οἰκονομέας.

CHAPTER XXXV

[*The inner meaning of Baptism. It is an imitation of Christ, a break with sin, and a prelude to our own resurrection. For those who lack the purification of baptism there is prepared the refining fire in the age to come.*]

THE descent into the water, and the triple immersion of the person in it, contains another mystery. For since the method followed in our salvation did not owe its efficacy so much to instruction imparted by teaching as to the very acts of Him Who entered into fellowship with man,[1] seeing that He has made life an accomplished fact, in order that, through the flesh which He assumed and at the same time deified,[2] all that is akin to it and of the same nature with it might therewith be saved, it was necessary that some method should be devised, by which the acts accomplished by him who follows might present some affinity and likeness to Him Who leads. We must see, then, what are the characteristics which the Author of our life was observed to possess, in order that, as the Apostle says,[3] the imitation of those who follow may be directed according to the pattern of the Captain of our salvation.

Those who are trained through what they see into rhythmical and orderly movement are led on to skill in arms by men well versed in military exercises, while he who fails to do what is shown to him remains devoid of

---

[1] Like Athanasius, Gregory regards the Death and Resurrection of Christ as representative and corporate acts. The starting-point of their teaching is Rom. vi. 3–11. See Moberly, *Atonement and Personality*, p. 356.

[2] συναποθεωθείσης. On the idea of "deification," see Inge, *Christian Mysticism*, App. C. p. 356 f.

[3] Heb. ii. 10. Gregory accepts the tradition of St. Paul's authorship.

such skill. In like manner they who have an equal zeal for what is good must follow by way of imitation Him Who leads us to our salvation, carrying out the actions which He has shown them. For it is not possible to attain the same end, unless they follow a similar route. Those who are incapable of threading the wanderings of labyrinths, if they fall in with some experienced person, and follow in his steps, succeed in traversing the various misleading windings of the building, whereas they would never have got through, had they not followed in the steps of their guide. So, I ask you, consider that the labyrinth of this life can never be threaded by human nature unless a man takes to that same path by which He Who entered into that life succeeded in passing outside its confining limits.

I use the word " labyrinth " figuratively to denote the prison of death from which there is no outlet, and in which the miserable race of mankind was confined. What, then, did we behold in the case of the Captain of our salvation? A state of death which lasted three days, and then a return to life. We must devise, then, something of the same kind, in our case too, that resembles this. What, then, is the device by which we may imitate that which was done by Him?

Everything that has become subject to death has its own appropriate abode fixed for it by nature, that is, the earth, in which it is laid and hidden away. Now earth and water have a close affinity to each other, for they are the only elements which have weight and tend downwards, and they alone abide in one another and are held by one another. Since, then, the death of the Author of our life led to burial in the ground, in virtue of the nature which He shared with us, the imitation of His death which we effect is represented in the neighbouring element. And as He, the Man from above,[1] assumed mortality, and after being laid beneath the earth returned

[1] John iii. 31; 1 Cor. xv. 47.

again to life on the third day, so every one who is united to Him in virtue of his bodily nature, having in view the same successful issue, I mean the goal of life, has water, instead of earth, poured upon him, and, passing beneath this element three separate times, reproduces the grace of the resurrection which was gained after three days.

In what precedes we have already indicated something of this kind, to the effect that the Divine providence introduced death into human nature with a special design, so that by the dissolution of body and soul vice may be drawn off and man may be refashioned again through the resurrection, sound, free from passion, pure, and without any admixture of evil. But in the case of the Author of our salvation the design for which death was appointed was fully attained, being completely carried out according to its special aim. For through death the elements which had been united were severed, and the elements which had been separated were again brought together, in order that, when our nature had been cleansed by the dissolution of elements which had been knit together, I mean body and soul, the return of the severed elements might be free from any alien admixture. But in the case of those who follow the Guide their nature does not permit an exact imitation in all points, but it admits now as much as it is capable of, while what is lacking it stores up for the time to come. In what, then, does this imitation consist? In effecting the disappearance of the vice mingled with our nature, represented in the image of mortification carried out by means of the water; it is not a complete disappearance, but a kind of break in the continuity of evil. For two causes contribute to the destruction of vice, the penitence of the sinner and the imitation of the death. By these means the man is, in a way, released from his connexion with evil, seeing that penitence leads him to hate vice and put it away, while death effects the destruction of evil.

But if it had been possible in this imitation to submit to death in its completeness, the result would have been not imitation, but identity of action, and evil would have wholly vanished from our nature, so that, as the Apostle says,[1] we should have " died unto sin once for all." But since, as we have said, we imitate the transcendent Power only so far as the poverty of our nature allows, by having water thrice poured upon us and rising again from the water, we represent that saving burial and the resurrection which took place in three days,[2] having this thought in our minds, that just as water is at our disposal, so that we may be immersed in it and rise again from it, in like manner He Who is the Ruler of the universe has it in His power to sink down into death, as we into the water, and to return again to His own proper state of blessedness.

If, then, we consider what is probable and judge the facts according to the capacity present in either case, we shall find no difference in the results, since each effects what is possible for him according to the standard of his nature. For just as it is possible for man to come into contact with the water without danger, if he wishes, with infinitely greater ease death lies within the reach of the Divine power, so that He may not only be immersed in it, but also experience in so doing no change involving weakness.

The reason, then, why it was necessary for us to rehearse beforehand the grace of the resurrection is this, that we might know that it is equally easy for us to be baptized with water and to rise again out of death. But in the ordinary events of life some things are primary in comparison with others, and without them there can be no success, although if the beginning be judged by the result, such beginning of the matter, when compared

[1] Rom. vi. 10.
[2] Cyril of Jerusalem similarly explains the significance of baptism. Cp. Rom. vi. 3-11.

with the result, will seem insignificant. For what equality
is there between a man and that which is implanted
with a view to the constitution of a living being? Yet
if the latter is absent, the former cannot come into being.
So also that which happens in the great resurrection,
superior though it is in nature, has its starting-point and
source here.[1] For it is not possible for that result to take
place, unless this has led the way. It is impossible, I
assert, that man can enter upon the resurrection without
the regeneration involved in the washing. And in saying
this I have not in view the remoulding and refashioning
of our concrete human nature; for to this our nature
must in any case attain, being impelled thereto by its
own fixed laws in accordance with the design of Him
Who so ordered it,[2] whether it receive the grace which
comes from the washing, or whether it remain excluded
from such initiation. But I have in view the restoration
to the blessed and divine state which is removed from
all affliction.

For not everything that is allowed the privilege of
returning to existence through the resurrection will
return to the same life, but there is a great interval
between those who have been purified and those who
lack purification. For those, in whose case the cleansing
effected through the washing has prepared the way, will
return to a life congenial to their state; and with that
which is pure freedom from passion is closely associated,
nor is there any doubt that blessedness consists in such
freedom from passion. But those whose natures have
been crusted over with passions, and in whose case no
means of cleansing the stain have been employed, no
sacramental water, no invocation of the Divine power,
no amendment based on penitence, must also, of necessity, be in their appropriate place. Now the appropriate

[1] *I. e.* in baptism.
[2] Gregory assumes the natural immortality of man. Cp.
Chaps. V, VIII.

place for gold which contains alloy is the refiner's fire,[1] in order that the vice which is mingled with them may be melted away, and their nature may, after long ages, be restored pure to GOD. Since, then, there is a kind of cleansing property in fire and water, they who have washed away the filth of vice through the sacramental water have no need of the other form of purification, whereas they who are not initiated into this method of purification are perforce purified by fire.

CHAPTER XXXVI

[The insignificance of the means by which baptism is effected, faith and water, is no measure of the greatness of the blessing which results from it, viz. kinship with GOD.]

THE general reason of mankind and the teaching of Scripture show that it is impossible for him who has not wholly washed away the stains of vice to enter in among the Divine company. This condition, slight as it is in itself, becomes the starting-point and foundation of great blessings. I call it slight because of the ease with which it is successfully fulfilled. For what difficulty is there in the matter, in believing that GOD is everywhere, and that being in all things He is present also with those who call upon His life-giving power, and being present He effects that which accords with His character. Now the characteristic of the Divine activity is the salvation of those who are in need. This salvation comes into operation through the purification in water. He who has been purified will participate in a state of purity, and

---

[1] Cp. Ch. XXVI, and see Introduction, p. 13 f. Gregory teaches a purification of the soul after the resurrection. His teaching has nothing in common with the later Western view of a purgatory in the intermediate state.

true purity is the Godhead. You see how slight a thing it is in its beginning and how easily accomplished; faith and water, the one lying within the power of our will, the other intimately connected with man's life. But how great and how good is the blessing which springs from them, the possession of kinship with the Deity Himself !

CHAPTER XXXVII

[In Baptism the soul is united to the Saviour by faith. In the Eucharist the body is brought into the same union, again through faith. How the One Body of Christ is given whole to thousands of believers. Illustration from the processes of nourishment and digestion. Christ plants Himself in the bodies of the faithful to raise them to incorruption.]

BUT since human nature has a twofold character, being compacted of soul and body, those who are being saved must by means of both lay hold of Him Who conducts them towards life. Now the soul being blended with Him by faith, derives therefrom the means of its salvation. For the union with life involves fellowship with life. But the body[1] comes into fellowship with its Saviour and is blended with Him in a different way. Those who have through treachery received poison neutralize its pernicious effect by another drug, but the

---

[1] In what follows Gregory appears to regard immortality as the chief benefit conferred upon the body by participation in the Eucharist. The germ of this idea is found in Ignatius' phrase (*Eph.*, 20) "medicine of immortality," applied to the Eucharist. On the connexion of this teaching with the Greek mysteries, see Inge, *Contentio Veritatis*, p. 294, and Lake, *Earlier Epistles of St. Paul*, pp. 212 ff., 233. Cp. John vi. 54, 58.

antidote, like the deadly drug, must pass within the vital organs of the individual, in order that the effect of the remedy may, in passing through them, be distributed through the whole body. So when we had tasted [1] of that which brought dissolution to our nature, of necessity we needed in turn something to reunite the severed elements, in order that such an antidote passing into us might by its own proper counteracting influence repel the mischief already introduced into the body by the poison.

What then is this? It is nothing else than that Body which was shown to be superior to death and which became the source of our life. For as a little leaven, according to the saying of the Apostle,[2] assimilates to itself the whole lump, so the Body, which was raised by GOD to immortality, by passing into our body transmutes and translates it to itself. For just as when a deadly drug is mingled with a healthy body, the whole of what is mingled with it becomes as worthless as the drug, so also that immortal Body passing into him that receives it transmutes the whole organism to its own nature.

Yet it is not possible for anything to penetrate the body, unless it is mingled with the vital organs by way of food and drink. Therefore the body must receive the life-giving power in the way that its nature permits. But since that Body which is the receptacle of Deity alone has received this grace,[3] and since it has been shown that it is not otherwise possible for our body to become immortal, unless it participates in immortality through fellowship with that which is immortal, it is fitting to consider how it became possible for that one Body, though continually distributed to so many myriads of believers throughout the whole world, to become in its entirety

---

[1] A reference to Gen. iii.
[2] 1 Cor. v. 6.
[3] *I. e.* " the life-giving power."

the possession of each, through the portion received, and yet to remain whole and entire.

In order, then, that our faith, with a view to logical consistency, may experience no hesitation in face of the question proposed for its consideration, it is fitting that our argument should turn aside for a moment to discuss the physiology of the body. For who is not aware that the nature of our body, considered in itself, does not possess life in a proper subsistence of its own, but maintains itself and continues in being through the influx of a force from without, by a ceaseless movement attracting to itself that which it lacks and casting off that which is superfluous? A leathern bottle full of some liquid, if the contents escape at the bottom, will not preserve its own shape about the volume, unless some other liquid in turn enters from above to fill up the void, so that he who sees the rounded circumference of this vessel knows that it does not belong to what he sees, but that it is the liquid flowing into it and contained in it which gives its shape to that which contains the volume. So also the constitution of our body has nothing that we can recognize of its own to maintain itself by, but continues in being by means of the force which is introduced into it.

Now this force is nourishment and bears that name. It is not the same for all bodies that are nourished, but each body has some appropriate nourishment assigned to it by Him Who directs its nature. For some living creatures are nurtured by digging up roots, others find their sustenance in herbs, others again feed on flesh, while man finds his chief sustenance in bread. In order to retain and preserve the element of moisture he has drink, not merely water alone, but water often sweetened with wine, in order to assist the element of heat within us. He who regards these elements, then, is regarding that which virtually constitutes the bulk of our body. For by passing into me those elements become body and blood, seeing that the nourishment by the power of assimilation is changed in each case into the form [1] of the body.

After thus investigating these points, we must bring back our thoughts to the problem before us. The question which we were asking was how that one Body of Christ gives life to all mankind, that is to all who have faith, being distributed amongst all and yet suffering no diminution in itself. Perhaps, then, we are not far from the probable explanation. It is admitted that the subsistence of the body is derived from nourishment, and that this nourishment is food and drink, and that in food bread is included, and in drink water sweetened with wine. It is admitted, further, that the Word of GOD, Who, as we explained at the beginning, is both GOD and Word, mingled with our human nature, and when He entered a body like ours, did not devise some other constitution for our nature, but provided for the continuance of His own body by the customary and appropriate means, maintaining its subsistence by food and drink, that food being bread. As then in our case, in accordance with what we have already frequently said, he that regards bread regards, in a way, the human body, for the former by passing into the latter becomes what it is, so in His case, too, the Body which was the receptacle of Deity, receiving the nourishment of bread, was, in some sense, identical with it, seeing that the nourishment, as we have said, was changed into the nature of the Body. For that which is characteristic of all men was recognized in that flesh also, that that Body, too, was maintained by bread, while the Body, through the indwelling of GOD the Word, was translated to the dignity of Godhead. With good reason, then, do we believe that

---

[1] εἶδος. Gregory has in mind the distinction between the " form " of matter and its " substance." The " form " remains unchanged, in spite of the continual flux of the material particles (στοιχεῖα).

now also the bread which is sanctified by the Word of
GOD [1] is transmuted into the Body of GOD the Word.
For that Body, too, was potentially bread, and it was
sanctified by the indwelling of the Word Who made His
tabernacle in the flesh.[2] The method, then, by which the
bread, which was transmuted in that Body, was changed
to Divine power, is the same method which yields now
the like result. For in that case the grace of the Word
sanctified the Body which derived its subsistence from
bread and, in a manner, was itself bread, whereas in
this case likewise the bread, as the Apostle says, is
sanctified by the Word of GOD and prayer, though it
is not by the process of being eaten that it advances to
the stage of becoming the Body of the Word, but it is
transmuted immediately into the Body through the
Word,[3] even as the Word has said, " This is my
Body." [4]

But all flesh is nourished also by the element of moisture, for without being combined with this the earthly
part of us cannot continue in life. As we maintain the
solid part of the body by solid and firm food, in like
manner we make an addition to the moist element from
the nature which is akin to it. And this, on entering our
bodies, is changed into blood by the faculty of assimilation, especially if through wine it receives the power of
being changed into heat. Since, then, that Flesh which
was the receptacle of Deity received this part also in
order to maintain itself in being, and the GOD Who
manifested Himself mingled Himself with our mortal

[1] 1 Tim. iv. 5. Gregory, like Origen, appears to interpret
the passage to refer to the personal Word.

[2] John i. 14.

[3] Gregory here teaches a change of " form " rather than
a change of substance. The constituent elements ($\sigma\tau o\iota\chi\epsilon\hat{\iota}a$)
of bread and wine are arranged under a new " form " ($\epsilon\hat{\iota}\delta os$)
and acquire fresh properties. The Western doctrine of
Transubstantiation moves in a different circle of ideas.

[4] Mark xiv. 22 (Matt. xxvi. 26; Luke xxii. 19).

nature in order that by communion with His Godhead
humanity might at the same time be deified, He plants
Himself, in accordance with His plan of grace, in all
believers by means of that Flesh, which derives its
subsistence from both wine and bread, mingling Himself
with the bodies of believers, in order that, by union
with that which is immortal, man also might participate
in incorruption. And this He bestows by virtue of the
blessing,[1] transforming [2] the nature of the visible elements
into that immortal thing.

CHAPTER XXXVIII

[The importance of a right faith for him who is baptized.]

OUR exposition, I think, has not omitted any of the
questions connected with our religion, except the treatment of faith. This we shall briefly expound in the
present treatise also. But for the benefit of those who
seek a more complete account we have already previously
expounded the subject in other works,[3] explaining the
matter in detail with all the care of which we were
capable. In those works we have not only engaged in
controversy with our opponents, but we have also independently considered the questions proposed to us. In
the present account we have thought it well to limit

---

[1] *I. e.* the " thanksgiving " of Mark xiv. 22 ; Matt. xxvi
26 ; I Cor. x. 16, from which the great Eucharistic prayer
of the Liturgies was developed.

[2] μεταστοιχειώσας. The word is used by Gregory in a
variety of senses : (1) of the change of the body after the
resurrection ; (2) of moral and spiritual changes. Hence its
use must not be pressed here to denote any particular kind
of change. The term, μετουσίωσις, was adopted at a much
later date as the equivalent for the Western *transubstantiatio*.

[3] *E. g.* the treatises *Against Eunomius*, and *On the Deity
of the Son and the Holy Spirit*.

ourselves, in speaking of faith, to that which is contained in the language of the Gospel,[1] namely that he who is begotten by the spiritual regeneration knows by whom he is begotten and what kind of living being he becomes. For this is the only kind of birth which has it in its power to become whatever it chooses.

CHAPTER XXXIX

[*The same continued. To believe that the Son and the Holy Spirit are created is to trust to an imperfect nature, which itself needs redemption, and so to impair the character of the new life in Baptism.*]

OTHER beings that are born owe their existence to the impulse of their parents, but the spiritual birth is dependent on the power of him who is being born. Since, then, the danger lies here, lest he should miss what is to his interest, seeing that the choice lies in every one's power, it is well, I say, that he who is eager for his own birth, should ascertain by consideration whom it will be to his advantage to have as a father, and from whom it will be best for him to derive the existence of his nature; for we have already said that a birth of this kind has it in its power to choose its parents. Since, then, existing things fall into two classes, the created and the uncreated, and since the uncreated nature possesses in itself unchangeableness and stability, while the created nature is subject to alteration and change, of which will he, who chooses with due reflection what is to his advantage, prefer to be the child, of that which is observed to be subject to change, or of that which possesses a nature that is unchanging, steadfast, and always consistent in goodness?

[1] Cp. John i. 13; iii. 6, 7.

H

In the Gospel, then, it has been handed down to us that there are three Persons [1] and Names [2] through Whom the birth is effected in believers, and he who is begotten in the Trinity is begotten equally by Father, Son, and Holy Spirit. For the Gospel speaks of the Spirit thus : " That which is born of the Spirit is spirit," [3] and Paul begets " in Christ," [4] and " the Father is Father of all." [5] Here, I pray, let the mind of the hearer show sobriety of judgment, lest it make itself the offspring of the unstable nature, when it is in its power to make the unchangeable and unalterable nature the Author of its own life. For that which is accomplished depends for its virtue on the disposition of heart in him who approaches the sacrament,[6] so that he who confesses that the holy Trinity is uncreated enters into the unchangeable and unalterable life, while he who is led by an erroneous conception to see in the Trinity the created nature, and then receives baptism in it, is again born into an existence which is subject to change and variation. For that which is born is perforce akin to the nature of its parents. Which, then, will be the more profitable, to enter into the unchangeable life or again to be tossed about in an unstable and variable existence ?

To every one who has the least particle of understanding it is plain that the stable is far more precious than the unstable, the perfect than that which is defective, that which lacks nothing than that which is lacking, that which admits of no advance but ever abides in the perfection of goodness than that which mounts upward by a gradual advance. He then who is a person of intelligence must in any case choose one of two alternatives, either to believe that the holy Trinity belongs to the uncreated nature, and so make it by means of the

---

[1] πρόσωπα.   [2] A reference to Matt. xxviii. 19.
[3] John iii. 6.   [4] 1 Cor. iv. 15.   [5] Cp. Eph. iv. 6.
[6] οἰκονομία, i. e. the " sacramental dispensation " of Chap. XXXIV.

spiritual birth the author of his own life, or, if he thinks that the Son and the Holy Spirit are external to the nature of the primal, true, and good GOD,[1] not to include belief in these Persons in the faith which he confesses at the time of his birth, lest, without knowing it, he cause himself to be adopted into the nature which is imperfect and needs some one to make it good, and in a way introduce himself again to a life of the same kind as his own, by withdrawing his faith from the transcendent nature.

For he who submits himself to any created thing unwittingly sets his hope of salvation on it and not on the Divine Being. For the whole creation, because it proceeds in an equal degree from non-existence to existence, is intimately connected in all its parts; and just as in the structure of the body all the members have a close affinity with one another, even though some happen to have a lower, and others a higher, position in the body; so created nature is a unity, in so far as it is created, and the difference between what is superior and what is inferior in us makes no division in its essential unity. For in the case of those things which we have previously thought of as coming alike out of a state of non-existence, even though they show a difference in other respects, we do not on this ground discover in them any variation of nature.

If, then, man is created, and if he thinks that the Spirit and the Only-begotten GOD are also created, he will be foolish to entertain the hope of a change for the better, seeing that he returns to himself. For that which happens in his case recalls the ideas of Nicodemus,[2] who, when he learned from the Lord the need of being born from above, because he had not yet grasped the meaning

---

[1] A reference to Eunomius, the leader of the extreme Arian party, whose teaching Gregory refutes in his work *Against Eunomius*.

[2] John iii. 4.

of the revelation, found himself led back by his thoughts to his mother's womb. So then if a man does not direct himself towards the uncreated nature, but towards the creation which is akin to him and shares his bondage, he belongs to the birth which is from below, not to that which is from above. Now the Gospel says that the birth of those who are saved is from above.[1]

CHAPTER XL

[*The regeneration in baptism is only effectual in those who put away sin. The rewards and punishments of GOD transcend anything in our experience. We must lay the foundations of future blessedness in this present life.*]

BUT up to this point in our treatment this catechetical instruction does not seem to me to be complete in its teaching. For we must, I think, consider also what follows this, because many of those who approach the grace of baptism neglect it, leading themselves astray in deception, and being born only in appearance and not in reality. For the transformation of our life which comes through regeneration will not be a transformation, if we continue in our present state. For I know not how it is possible to imagine him who remains in the same state to have become some one different, when none of his characteristics have undergone a transformation. For it is clear to everybody that the object in view in receiving the saving birth is the renewal and change of our nature. Yet humanity in itself does not admit of a change as the result of baptism; neither the power of rational thought, nor the faculty of understanding, nor the capacity for

---

[1] John iii. 3.

exact knowledge, nor any other of the special characteristics of human nature undergo a change. For the
change would assuredly be for the worse, if any one of
these particular features of our nature were replaced by
something else. If, therefore, the birth from above is a
kind of refashioning of the man, and these characteristics
admit of no change, we must consider what change it is
which makes the grace of regeneration effective.

Clearly it is when the evil characteristics of our nature
have been blotted out that the change for the better
takes place. If, then, as the prophet says,[1] having been
" washed " in this sacramental washing, we become
" clean " in our wills, having washed away the " iniquities
of our souls," we become better and are transformed to
a better state   Whereas, if the washing is applied to
the body, while the soul does not wash away the stains
of its passions, but the life after initiation is of the same
character as the uninitiate life, even though it be a
bold thing to say, yet I will say it and not draw back,
in such cases the water is water, and the gift of the Holy
Spirit nowhere appears in what takes place, whenever
not only the deformity of anger dishonours the Divine
image, or the passion of covetousness, and the uncon-
trolled and unseemly thought, and pride, envy, conceit,
but also when a man retains in his possession the gains
made by injustice, and the woman whom he has made
his own by adultery continues to minister to his pleasures
even after baptism. If these and the like vices mark
the life of him who has been baptized after, no less than
before, I cannot see how he has been changed ; for I behold
the same man as I formerly did. He who has suffered
injustice, he who has been falsely accused, he who has
been thrust out of his own possessions, these, for their
part, see no change in the man who has been washed.
They have not heard from his lips the words of Zacchæus :
" If I have taken anything from any man by false accusa-

[1] Isa. i. 16.

tion I restore fourfold." [1] The things which they used to say of him before baptism, the same they still recount of him in full. They call him by the same names, an extortioner, covetous of others' goods, one who lives luxuriously on other men's misfortunes. Let him, then, who continues in the same state, and who in spite of that keeps prating to himself of the change for the better effected in him through baptism, listen to the words of Paul: [2] "If a man think himself to be something, when he is nothing, he deceives himself." For that which you have not become, you are not. "As many as received Him," the Gospel says [3] of those who have been regenerated, "to them gave He the right to become children of God." He who has become the child of any one undoubtedly is akin to his parent. If, then, you have received God and become a child of God, show by the aim of your life the God Who is in you, show in yourself Him Who has begotten you. The characteristics by which we recognize God are those by which he who has become a son of God ought to show his relationship to God: "He openeth His hand and filleth every living thing with His good pleasure"; [4] "He passeth over iniquities"; [5] "He repenteth Him of evil"; [6] "The Lord is gracious to all, [7] and bringeth not on us His wrath every day"; [8] "God is an upright Lord, and there is no unrighteousness in Him"; [9] and all the like characteristics which we are taught by passages scattered throughout the Scriptures. If you share these characteristics, you have in truth become a child of God. But if you persist in exhibiting the characteristics of vice, it is in vain for you to babble to yourself of your birth from above. Prophecy will tell you that you are "a son of

---

[1] Luke xix. 8.   [2] Gal. vi. 3.
[3] John i. 12.   [4] Ps. cxlv. 16.
[5] Micah vii. 18 (LXX.).   [6] Joel ii. 13.
[7] Ps. cxlv. 9.   [8] Ps. vii. 12 (LXX.).
[9] Ps. xcii. 14.

man," not "a son of the Most High." You "have pleasure in vanity," [1] you "seek a lie." You have not learned in what way man "is magnified," [2] that it can only be by becoming holy.

To this teaching we must add a further point which remains to be dealt with, that the blessings which in the Gospels are set before those who have lived well are such as cannot be outlined in any description. For how can we describe "things which neither eye hath seen, nor ear hath heard, and which have not entered into the heart of man "? [3] Neither has the painful life of sinners any equal in any of the things which in this world afflict the senses. But even though we use terms familiar to us here to denote some of the chastisements inflicted there, the difference is by no means slight. When you hear the word fire,[4] you have been taught to conceive of it as a fire different from the fire we know, because to that fire there is added something which is not in this. For that fire "is not quenched," but experience has devised many means of quenching this fire, and the difference between the fire which is quenched and that which does not admit of being quenched is great. Hence it is something different, and not identical with this. Again, when we hear of a "worm" we must not let our thoughts be carried away by the identity of the word with this earthly creature. For the addition "that dieth not" suggests the thought that it is a different kind of being from that which we know. Since, then, these are the things which are held out to our expectation in the after-life, as the natural growth and outcome in our life of each man's bent of character, according to the righteous judgment of GOD, it will be the mark of sober wisdom to look not to the present, but to the

[1] Cp. Ps. iv. 2; lxxxii. 6, 7.
[2] Ps. iv. 4 (LXX.).
[3] 1 Cor. ii. 9.
[4] Cp. Isa. lxvi. 24; Matt. iii. 12; Mark ix. 43 f.

future, and in this short and fleeting life to lay the foundations of that ineffable blessedness, and by a good choice keep ourselves free from all experience of evil, now in this present life, and hereafter when we win our eternal reward.

GENERAL INDEX

ALLEGORY, allegorical inter-
pretation, 13, 46, 94
Amphilochius, 17
Anomœans, 8, 23, 24. See
Eunomius, Arians.
Anselm, *Cur deus homo*, 17
Apollinaris, 9, 84
Apologists, Christian, 12
Arians, 8, 9, 10, 17, 115.
See Eunomius, Anomœans.
Aristotle, 18, 35, 98
Athanasius, 15 f., 17, 59, 66,
67, 79, 87, 92, 94, 101
Atonement, 16 f., 69 f.
Augustine, 95

Baptism, 17, 19, 97 f., 101 f.
Basil, Bishop of Cæsarea, 7,
8, 12, 13
Basilides, 23
Body, the human, 14, 46

Catechists, Christian, 11
Christ, two natures of, 9,
54
Christianity, spread of, 67
Clement of Alexandria, 12,
46
Coats of skin, 14, 46
Colson, F. H., 11, 61, 64
Creation of man, 9, 10, 14,
35 f.
Cross (Crucifixion) of Christ,
15, 92 f.
Cyril of Jerusalem, 104

Death, place of, in Divine
providence, 14, 46 f., 103 f.;
of Christ, 15, 92
Deification of man, 15, 101,
112
Demons, belief in, 66

Eucharist, 18 f., 107 f.
Eucharistic prayer, 112
Eunomius, 8, 9, 10, 112, 115
Euthymius Zigabenus, 11
Evil, negative character of,
13, 18, 37 f., 44; origin of,
10

Faith, 10, 17, 107, 110,
112 f.
Fall of man, 9, 10, 38 f.
" Form " and " substance,"
110
Forbes, G. H., 21
Free-will, 10, 13, 37, 44, 89 f.,
91 f.
Fronto Ducæus, 20

Gallandi, 20
Gelasian Sacramentary, 76
Germanus, Patriarch of Con-
stantinople, 11
Glover, T. R., 66
God, knowledge of, 18. See
Immanence ; Transcend-
ence.
Greek theology, 12, 17
Gregory the Great, 78

INDEX OF WORDS